NAKED

WITHOUT A NETWORK

MORE IMPORTANT THAN
WHO YOU KNOW IS *WHO KNOWS YOU*

DAVIS R. BLAINE

- TESTIMONIALS -

Davis Blaine is truly a maven when it comes to the tried-and-true techniques of networking. Whether you're new to business development or simply looking for a fresh perspective, *Naked Without a Network* will help you step up your game.

David Ackert
President, The Ackert Advisory

Davis Blaine's book is an excellent primer on how to develop and maintain a business network. Drawing from his many years organizing and operating ProVisors in Southern California, Blaine provides an easy-to-read, practical approach for anyone who needs a starting place for business development. In addition, for someone like me, who has been "pounding the pavement" for a while, Blaine's book gave me some new ideas and reminded me of projects I could incorporate into my networking.

Joel J. Berman
Partner, Jeffer Mangels, Butler & Mitchell LLP

My good friend Davis Blaine has shared with us his many years of networking experience, wisdom, and lessons learned by his watching, teaching, and most importantly, doing. He is one of the most connected people I know, and in this book, he shows us how to build our own networks and create our own lifeline in the process.

I am genuinely appreciative that he has taken the time to share his knowledge effectively and succinctly.

Neil R. Finestone

CEO, Finestone Partners

It's not often that you can get into the brain of a master networker. Davis Blaine, founder of one of the most successful networking organizations in America, opens his heart in *Naked Without a Network* and takes the reader by the hand, revealing what it takes to become an expert communicator. This book is for everyone, particularly students and people who want to succeed socially and professionally. I wish I had this book when I was just starting out. But no matter where you are in your career, spending time with *Naked Without a Network* will make you a more interesting, happier, and successful person.

Peter K. Studner, Author of *Super Job Search IV*, President of

Peter K. Studner Associates, Inc., Career Transition Management

No one knows more about networking than Davis Blaine. After all, he founded one of the most successful, prestigious networking organizations in the country. In this thoughtful, user-friendly book, Davis shares secrets and best practices he mastered (and often created) in dozens of years of networking at the highest level. Anyone who's serious about growing a professional practice <u>needs</u> to read this book.

Doug Levinson

Strategy That Rocks

- DEDICATION -

The inspiration and perspiration needed to write a book is surreal, like a wave in the ocean. It teases you just enough to get you started. Then it leaves for a period of time, only to return and leave again. When an author finally commits to sharing in written form, he will labor for intense blocks of time. I liken this activity to Newton's First Law of Motion: an object at rest stays at rest and an object in motion stays in motion with the same speed and in the same direction unless acted upon by an unbalanced force.

This dedication is to the "balanced" forces in my life that have encouraged me to complete this tome. My first book, *Coach Daddy*, was inspired by my experiences in coaching my kids. The triggering event to write this book was the sale of the network group that I started and built over the course of three decades.

First, I thank my adoring wife. She provided the stability, encouragement, and love, which allowed me to spend the "creative" time thinking and writing.

Kudos to my son Justin, who provided cogent ideas, revisions, and editorial assistance. He made this more personal, helping me tell the whole story of my evolution. My daughter Whitney provided the final substantive editing and really polished this work.

To my other children, Tristan, Brittara, and daughter-in-law Melissa, for their love and support.

Other significant contributors, in terms of content, concept, and edits, were friends and fellow professionals: Marc Hankin, Neil Finestone, Joel Berman, David Ackert, Shel Brucker, and John

Ambrecht. The production team included my very capable and collaborative assistant, Alen Ohanian.

A special thanks to marketing guru Brian Hemsworth, whose creative insight and inspiration spurred me to unexpected heights.

- Table of Contents -

- FOREWORD -

By Mark Goulston

In the world of business relationships, it is less important who you know than who knows you and how they know you. You will find no better guide to making valuable introductions and generating referrals than what you are now holding in your hands.

As an experienced book author, I know when reading a book how much of an author's essence is in between the covers. This book is the most complete treatise on the wide-ranging topic of networking and building relationships that I have read. In addition, I am pleased to have known Davis Blaine for nearly 25 years. I know that he put his soul into building a model network organization, and that is exhibited in *Naked Without a Network*.

I have been a member of the aforementioned PNG organization for many years. Davis and I have discussed at length the issues he faced to continually deliver meaningful benefits to a varied group of professional service providers. The organization succeeded so well that Davis could sell his interest in 2013.

The process of developing lasting connections within a community is an art, not a science. This book provides numerous suggestions for anyone to create his or her own network. Davis built an entirely new culture and systematic approach to networking, while at the same time using this solid referral base to enhance and grow his professional practice.

There is no substitute for giving freely to others. This approach makes us feel good about ourselves, while also attracting others to us. One of the best ways to succeed in business and life is to become a center of influence. When you give value to another by paying it forward, you will create a karma–like state of being.

In this book, Davis provides an untold number of ideas for anyone to start and plan a lifestyle of authentic relationship building. As he clearly identifies, the buck starts with each person. No two paths to successful networking are the same—perhaps similar, but not the same. If the reader adapts even a few of the specific nuggets, his subsequent path will be both enjoyable and profitable.

Davis has done his homework and research, which supports his easy-to-apply concepts. Thus, this book resonates with anyone, no matter the career—a policeman, politician, or businessman. At some point in our lives, each of us is vulnerable to difficulty or failure. Each of us needs a community that can support us during these times, as well as the good ones. Deeply participating in and contributing to our various circles of friends and colleagues is the best prescription for significantly reducing our vulnerability to life. At the end of the day, we get to create the life we want.

Naked Without a Network — don't leave home or your office without it.

- PREFACE -

This book covers my evolution from having no network in 1987 to having an extensive one today. Creating and maintaining strong, effective relationships is not just a lofty intention; rather, it is a necessity for a fulfilling career, as well as a satisfying personal life.

This book is not just for professionals or corporate executives. Rather, it is for anyone and everyone who wants to be relevant in their chosen occupation, charity, or community.

I have devoted much of the last 27 years to pursuing the keys to building authentic and lasting relationships, largely in the form of business networking. Done right and well, networking results in trusting connections and usually in some form of friendship. Since my enlightened discovery of the power of networking in 1988, I have learned many invaluable lessons and life-altering traits. Yet, I continue to learn new information vital to the natural flow of relationship building. A large part of this effort is creating good karma, or putting forth yourself to help others. However, it is not all giving without knowing how to properly receive.

Authentic networking is not telling or selling. Thus, it should not be threatening to those involved in the process. However, enter a time capsule with me and let's go back to 1988. What was the general mindset about networking at that time? There were very few active groups, and they were looked at askance. While people needed activities and places to make connections, those who considered themselves professional and/or relatively powerful business persons thought they had no use for an organized network. At that time, the organized groups were places for selling to one another. They lacked a culture of giving and helping others.

In the late 1980s and even the early 1990s, most people did not have positive networking experiences; there was no clear pattern or model of success to follow. Although I was a novice at responsible connecting, I created a networking philosophy and format that many other groups have adopted. It is the way professional service providers should interact. That beginning resulted in a business (originally named Professionals Network Group or PNG, which is now known as ProVisors) that redefined network organizations. Throughout this book are references to the PNG/ProVisors system and tenets. And, the impetus for this organization was my own lack of a network when I started a valuation and appraisal business in late 1987.

I was truly "naked without a network." The only way to build my business was to first build relationships–a referral network. There's one expression that applies to this scenario: Necessity is the Mother of Invention. While this network helped others who joined, it also helped me build relationships. The unintended but wonderful consequence was that ProVisors became a successful, stand-alone business.

- INTRODUCTION -

How do you start a business without any sources of revenue? Perhaps, the better question is "why"? I did not ask myself either of these questions when I started my valuation business in 1987.

Little did I know how difficult it would be to establish myself, even with nearly 20 years' experience in the valuation industry. With virtually no local connections, I was "naked without a network."

Instinctively, I applied what I knew with unrelenting fervor. I focused on helping others before asking for anything in return. That form of giving was manifested by my connecting peer professionals to one another. As a result of this intensive connecting, I created a network organization known as Professionals Network Group (PNG).

By the time I sold PNG (then ProVisors) in mid-2013, my experiences and learnings were equivalent to a Ph.D. in interpersonal relations. I then decided to write this book and share what had helped me build PNG and two other successful businesses.

One important lesson I learned during the many years of managing PNG is that networking is a contact sport. What is most important is that you reach out to make those contacts. Done well, it is like a ballet. Done poorly, it can be detrimental to your career.

The road to building your network begins here. Use this book as an ultimate reference guide to map your plan. I hope the many and specific concepts presented in this book will be useful in your journey. Remember, it is a marathon not a sprint.

Chapter 1

LIFE BEGINS

Success is how high you bounce when you hit bottom.
—George Smith Patton, Jr.

The process of relationship building was like a new beginning to my life. For me, it started nearly 30 years ago. This book is about me overcoming that nearly fatal position of starting a company without a solid network. In 1987, my "network" was almost non-existent. Figuratively, I was "naked without a network."

Developing a networking is a journey and a progression that continues today, and actually only gets better with time. The more we know about ourselves and what we want to do with our lives, the better equipped we are for the lifestyle that comes with continuous networking.

I have read numerous books and spoken to a countless number of people about networking and building relationships. Each person has a different style and approach. One element common to all of them is that networking is a continuum; it is an ongoing and evolving process. Each person must clearly define his or her mindset and attitude toward networking, and what it means to him or her. That is the most likely approach to tangible success. You can read and learn and listen to other people. But at the end of the day, it's really how you perceive the benefits and mechanics of positive networking and how you will apply those tactics in your everyday life.

Provided in this book are many ideas for professional service providers and corporate executives to help build their communities/networks. These principles are applicable to every human being in any circumstance, whether a teacher, policeman, union laborer, housewife (or house husband), etc.

What I believe to be one of the more fascinating aspects of good networking is that it can begin when you decide to start the process. The saying, "This is the first day of the rest of your life," is completely applicable for entering into a lifetime of positive (authentic) networking. Nearly every person has experienced or will experience the essence of great relationship building, which is why people gravitate to like-minded communities. There are many different forms, but nearly all are based on common links to one another. No two people in a community think and act just like every other person in that community. However, there is a common bond, linkage, mission, or some reasonable purpose that binds each participant to the community, and keeps them engaged and invested.

The power of networking and building incredibly positive relationships cannot be understated. I learned this lesson the hard way, which is probably why I am so passionate about sharing the best practices and mindset necessary for the right type of networking.

Being a net giver and a person who is continually open to helping others is the most positive and powerful force on this planet.

Early Career

I have been a professional service provider — involving valuations, appraisals, and investment banking — for more than

40 years. In the early days of my career, there were very few formal networking communities. Other than alumni groups, country clubs, religious institutions, non-profit organizations, Rotary, and some informal gatherings, there were no formal networking organizations known to me. None of the aforementioned is considered a focused business networking community. These institutions or groups did not typically meet for the purpose of exchanging commerce. While business occurred and personal friendships were built, it was more by happenstance and less as a planned outcome. In fact, some clubs frowned upon "networking," believing it was contrived selling to one another. That is not to say that people weren't making solid connections in those organizations. Some business executives, who are typically isolated working in their companies, join industry or market associations. These latter groups were formed for the purpose of sharing information throughout an industry sector and also for executive connections.

Two years after starting my first job in 1969, four of us left to start our own company, American Valuation Consultants (AVC). This firm was based in Chicago. As an owner of a valuation and appraisal firm, my primary duties involved managing staff, including sales people, and developing new clients for business. Our target customers or clients were middle market or large companies, usually businesses larger than $30 million in revenue. These firms would hire appraisal companies to value their tangible and intangible assets, as well as estimate value for the business. Many of these valuations and appraisals were done for mergers and acquisitions, as well as defending the taxpayer's position against the Internal Revenue Service or Securities and Exchange Commission (SEC).

In the 1970s and 1980s, much like today, it was important for me to fully understand the client. So I made a point of getting to know the other professionals serving those same companies. For example, I always tried to meet or know of the company's auditors and legal counsel. At the same time, there were very few valuation and appraisal companies. Contacting companies directly (cold calling) was an accepted mode of "selling", versus relying on other trusted advisors to refer us into the company. Thus, the most direct mode of marketing to these companies was to call the executives, such as the treasurer, tax manager, or chief financial officer. Often, these contacts provided direct access into a company, in lieu of being referred in by another professional.

AVC grew nicely in the 1970s to a nearly $10 million revenue firm. In 1978, one of the original founders, Dan Richter, and I bought out the other two primary shareholders, Bill Hawkins and Larry Gooch, who moved to Los Angeles. Subsequently, in 1981 Bill and Larry approached Arthur D. Little (ADL), a Massachusetts-based consulting firm, to capitalize a valuation and appraisal company. ADL was comprised more than 2,000 consultants worldwide.

Dan and I were approached in mid-1979 to sell AVC to another firm. Since Dan was tired of his management role, I reluctantly agreed to sell. Although the price was reasonable, I wanted to stay and grow the practice. By this time, I had developed a small network cadre of trusted professional advisors in and around Chicago. Reflecting on the people and professionals I knew well, the contact list was very small. I was guilty of working in and not on my business. I sold the business in late 1979 and moved to Los Angeles, where I had always wanted to live.

In the early 1980s, I noticed a change in this style of directly contacting prospects. The well-known, larger manufacturers were not growing. The country was shifting from a manufacturing-centric economy to one comprised of more service companies. Manufacturing and production were moving offshore, amid the advent of startups and technology-based firms in the U.S. This proliferation in the number of smaller to middle market firms was accompanied by a parallel growth in professional service providers, including valuation and appraisal practitioners. In addition, there were much smaller companies now requiring the services of professionals.

From 1980 to 1983, I was president of the successor firm, Valuation Research (VRC). I traveled throughout the United States, which made it difficult to maintain many contacts in Los Angeles. I would characterize those three years as the "place holder in my career." While I was in charge of all of the operations, as well as developing new clients in L.A, I was an employee with no real ownership. I even debated leaving the valuation business. In fact, I actually pursued more than a few acquisitions of small businesses, mostly in manufacturing.

Near the end of my consulting agreement with VRC, I reconnected with Bill and Larry about joining Arthur D. Little Valuation (ADLV). They welcomed me into the top management ranks, since they needed help to grow the company. I served four years as chief operating officer, responsible for managing the many offices outside of L.A. Going to work at Arthur D. Little Valuation (ADLV) in 1983 was a major shift from my prior life of running a smaller, entrepreneurial valuation and appraisal firm. However, I gained important perspective from working at two vastly different companies.

In the '80s, the ADLV salespersons were actively connecting with other professional service providers. Since ADLV was a national valuation firm, meeting with larger accounting and law firms was a natural course of action. The clients operated in a similar space. We were trusted advisors coordinating with major companies. A few examples of larger clients included General Motors, Chevron, Hewlett Packard, Turner Broadcasting, and IBM. When I started my own firm in 1987, I knew my targeted clientele would be vastly different, both in size and type.

Since my main function at ADLV was managing all of our offices, I was travelling all the time. In addition, while living in the Los Angeles area where we were headquartered, I did not have direct prospecting or client closing responsibilities. My efforts were devoted to training others how to prospect for and bring in clients, as well as managing a staff of nearly 350 people. In early

1987, Price Waterhouse approached our parent company, Arthur D. Little, about buying ADLV. We thought we might become part of a major accounting firm. It was at this time in 1987 that the Big Six (the six largest accounting firms in the world) were buying consulting practices to augment their audit and tax services. ADLV, the first or second largest valuation and appraisal firm in the world at that time, was a viable target. However, the buyout did not occur. While we had many competent professionals, Price Waterhouse believed there were significant and disruptive politics throughout the middle and lower ranks.

The only reason to look back at prior decisions is to reflect on how we might improve our decision-making now.

Soon after the failed buyout, I knew it was time to start my own business, The Mentor Group. I could look back to 1983 when I took the job as the chief operating executive at ADLV and bemoan the fact that I did not start The Mentor Group (TMG) then. However, my mindset in 1983 was not oriented to starting another company, much as I had done in 1971. The right time to start anything is really the time at which it is started. That is why there is no good or bad time to start your networking process. The best time is today.

"Your vision will become clear only when you look into your heart. Who looks outside, dreams. Who looks inside, awakens." *Carl Jung.*

$6,348.03

$6,348.03 was the monthly mortgage payment on the new house my wife and I built in 1987. In fact, we experienced three of life's five most stress-inducing events, all in one day. On October 7,

1987, we moved into a new home, brought our third child home from the hospital, and started a new company — a perfect trauma trifecta. Oh, and we were nearly broke.

To compound matters, I was "naked without a network." My rolodex was not just bleak; it was nearly void of any useful contacts. I literally had to "go to work" to create a sustainable number of referring professionals just to keep my company afloat.

I believe that I survived, and ultimately thrived, by digging deep inside myself so I would not fail at my new venture, only to also create a totally new and profitable networking organization. I could not have succeeded without the constant and unswerving support of my wife, Karen. Whenever I need an honest critique or solution to a dilemma, she is my objective sounding board. In the following fable, the Emperor could have used that honest feedback about his clothing.

Many years ago, there was an Emperor so fond of new clothes that he spent all of his time and money on being well-dressed. The only reason he spent time reviewing his soldiers or attending the theatre was to show off his new clothes. In fact, he had a different coat for every hour of the day. He was described or heralded as "the Emperor's in his dressing room."

Every day strangers came to his city. On one such occasion, two swindlers posed as weavers. They promised him that their colors and fabrics were so fine that they became invisible to anyone unfit for his office, or who was unusually stupid. The Emperor could not wait for them to outfit him.

The weavers stole all of the finest silks and put them in their travel bags, as they worked the empty looms into the night. The Emperor was wild with anticipation of the finest clothing; townspeople knew of the cloth's magical power and wanted to find out which neighbors were stupid.

In great anticipation, the Emperor sent his honest old minister to check on the weavers and their progress. The minister was flummoxed that he could not see the cloth, believing himself stupid and unfit to serve as minister. So he told his Emperor the patterns and colors were beautiful. Then, the Emperor sent another trustworthy advisor to check on the progress. Not wanting to appear stupid, he praised the material he did not see.

Finally, the Emperor brought these two trusted advisors (early definition of a latter day phenomena) and others to see the empty looms. He too was flabbergasted that he saw nothing. However, too scared to admit he might be unfit for his kingdom, he exclaimed the clothes were magnificent and unsurpassed. He agreed to wear them in the procession.

All of his servants made motions as if to carry his train, since no one wanted to admit to the truth. In the middle of the procession, a little child exclaimed, "But he hasn't got anything on." And the town cried out that he was naked. Not to be outdone, though he knew they were right, he continued to the end as proud as ever.

There I was, just like the Emperor, "naked without a network." And I had to quickly assimilate so many professionals in a short time. I could only hope that few people saw me as vulnerable.

In the early years of my career, when I had more direct client responsibility, I was a trusted financial advisor to my clients, especially on matters such as valuations and acquisitions. And I knew their trusted advisors. That was not close to my situation before I started The Mentor Group.

In early October 1987, I checked my Rolodex for potential contacts (somewhat working backwards, after having already started a business). At that time, it contained about six names. The obvious reason for my complete lack of contacts was two-fold:

1. I did not understand the true mechanics and/or genius of networking.

2. I was completely focused on and in the business of ADLV, travelling to its various offices throughout the United States. Thus, my time and effort was focused on the people who I was managing and training, and not my contacts.

I had a major dilemma: how do I build a business in Los Angeles knowing only six contacts? I was determined not to get on airplanes and connect with the few people that I had met in various cities throughout the United States. I needed an efficient way to meet as many people in the greater Los Angeles area, as fast as I could. The expression, "Necessity is the Mother of Invention," was completely apt in my circumstances in late 1987. Fortunately, one of the people in my limited Rolodex was glad to connect with me. He provided us a major valuation assignment, which started our firm on a solid footing. However, I still needed to develop my own extensive network to create an ongoing source of revenue.

One day I was invited to attend a meeting which included many professional service providers. We had an interesting discussion about organizing a group to share information and contacts. In addition to attending this meeting, which gave me some good ideas for organizing future groups, I was spending nearly 100 percent of my time in personal meetings with professional advisors. This outreach activity was part of my primary role to get new clients, since I was supported by senior valuation professionals performing the services. At each of those one-on-one meetings, I would offer them contacts that might help them, as well as asking for as many new names as they would share with me. While it is much easier today with modern technology to share contacts, somehow I was able to garner enough contacts and phone numbers to be able to set up meetings with many professionals in a short period of time. In those days, I usually had a minimum of three to five meetings per day. I was quickly establishing contacts with other experienced professionals, and providing them my list of contacts that could help them. It then occurred to me that I was in the minority of people that were following this path to building a database. Also, I was developing a reputation as a person who was willing to share with others.

Shared Value Proposition

As I built my list of contacts, I began to focus on those persons who were the better trusted advisor professionals. Other traits I considered included character, trustworthiness, and personality. I was beginning to identify those traits in trusted advisors who would form the cornerstone for my network organization.

What was my method for setting up meetings? I never made cold calls. Some were warmer than others, but leads or new contacts were always by referral. Just as I passed along names and phone numbers (remember, there was no World Wide Web yet, nor was email as robust as it is today) of potential links, I also received the same. Using another person's name was the key to opening the next door. What was my general process for conducting a meeting? What follow-up did I deliver to these contacts? My approach was simple and has not changed much to this day.

1. Learn about him as a person – family, passions, philosophy, etc.

2. Ask first about his practice and specialty.

3. Find out about his client focus, such as industry, size, type of matter, etc.

4. Briefly and clearly explain your main service offerings. Interject specific client examples and stories to illustrate how your services dovetail.

5. Allow him to ask questions about your services.

6. Ask how you can help him, such as suggesting contacts that might be good direct links for business.

7. Explain the importance and impact of gathering in groups to share ideas and learn about each other (forerunner of an organization like ProVisors).

The above is only a guide for how a typical conversation might evolve. Obviously, the more interactive and personal the discourse, the faster and deeper you get to know one another, and the sooner you determine if you will work together in some capacity.

So what is my value proposition? It is not that our staff of senior professionals is so much better than any competitor. I cannot prove that. I can say with pride and conviction that no one is better than us; but that is not the only reason people want to do business with us. Why might clients and advisors remember us? Because we always offer something of value to them beyond the basic services.

By mid-1988, I had enough contacts to begin organizing groups comprised of my resources and professionals, as well as their contacts. In these early days of networking, the format was rather simple. Each of us had an opportunity to give a very brief introduction or elevator speech (conveying a clear, simple message in the time it takes to go from the ground floor to floor 10 of an office building). The rest of the meeting was usually someone throwing out a discussion topic and other people participating in the conversation.

The first host was Ernst & Young in Century City, California. Business cards were made for every person in attendance to encourage them to make contacts between monthly meetings.

From this early, rudimentary type of networking group, I parlayed those initial group meetings and my other contacts into building 11 groups over the next two years. Those 11 groups formed the basis for what became Professionals Network Group, now known as ProVisors. In late 1989, I met Gordon Gregory. He and a handful of others were keenly interested in what I was building. I was not even sure what I was creating at the time, but it felt right. High-level professionals returned to the monthly meetings on a regular basis. A community was formed by the professionals who regularly attended their respective group or guested at another nearby group. There were no rules or restrictions. The hosts were service firms with a large conference room (no cost); each host provided coffee and bagels or sweets. I moderated all of the groups and sent out reminder notices by fax of the upcoming meeting. Yes, by fax!

Toward the end of 1990, I recognized that I needed help in managing the network. Not only did I own and operate The Mentor Group, but in 1989, I had acquired 75 percent of a lighting company in Hollywood. While my partner, who acquired 25 percent, ran the day-to-day, I often visited the company to look after my investment.

To select a partner for the no-name network, I interviewed three people. Gordon was the only one who showed the initiative and intuition for building an organization. We incorporated in 1991 as Professionals Network Group, often called PNG.

Difficult 90s

Initially, we had to overcome an early 1990s recession, which lasted well into 1994. The model of business decorum in a network setting was quite unique at that time. Outright "selling" to other members was not only verboten, but openly chastised. In the early 90s, we were breaking new ground, unlike during the start of the recession in 2007 and 2008 when our networking model was well-known and accepted, and professionals needed to build relationships.

By 1992, when PNG started charging dues, PNG was one of four significant "network" organizations that I knew in Los Angeles. Ivan Misner had started an organization called Business Network International (BNI) in 1986. The format and the type of participant were similar but uniquely different than PNG. The other organizations that had staying power in L.A. were LAVA, Los Angeles Venture Association, and Association for Corporate Growth (ACG). Each of these latter two organizations arranged monthly meetings of 75 to 150 people in a large mixer setting. Often, the program consisted of a speaker(s), seminar, or panel presentation. At the same time, there was no emphasis in either of these latter organizations about getting together after the mixer/meeting to build relationships. People were merely left to their own devices to figure that out. Much to their credit, BNI organized small groups of 15 to 20 participants. They held weekly meetings, but did not allow any competitors in the same group. Rather than having different types of lawyers, usually only one lawyer was allowed to join. In addition, BNI's focus was on local merchants, much as a Chamber of Commerce or Rotary Club would be organized. The group consisted of a variety of professions or businesses, such as a dentist, car mechanic, accountant, etc.

Since we were creating a new paradigm for networking and relationship building, there was no other model to even contrast and compare against. At the same time, the growth of membership was frustratingly slow. Yet, I knew we were on the right track with PNG. I had many meetings with members that confirmed the stickiness of the vision, methods, and benefits. At one point in the mid-1990s, Gordon seriously considered abandoning the organization and giving it to some members who wanted to operate it. I knew that was giving in and giving up. Obviously, that was not an option for me. It probably drove me harder to make it work and work very well. My wife and I discussed the ProVisors tribulations, and she was steadfast in her belief that it was a great business model. She knew well that my connections in PNG were driving valuation referrals.

One of the key changes to PNG that had a dramatic impact on growth in membership was a decision in 1995 to enlist and empower members to become group leaders. The effect on member acceptance and participation was significant. The organization was no longer viewed as the "Davis and Gordon show."

Throughout the 1990s, I continued to meet many professionals, inviting most of them to attend a PNG meeting. However, it was still a third business, secondary to the valuation and investment banking practices I owned. Dues rose slowly, as we grappled with correlating the charge for membership with the benefits. Similar to promoting employees to managers or officers, these first group leaders really assumed responsibility for building groups of quality members. They took "ownership" in the organization, believing that this position would enhance their relationships and grow their business. Circa 1999, we hired a full-time person as an administrator. We started to automate the record keeping and announcements to members.

The groups were used as incubators. I would try something new, and share it with other group leaders if it worked. We were learning on the fly, continuing to add benefits like organization-wide mixers, the ability to guest at other groups, etc. Allowing members to guest at all the groups three times per year accelerated the connectivity and commerce. This policy also created a larger community of interrelated professionals, so members felt less isolated as part of a home group. Our member "surveys" on how well we were doing were often done in person. Like any good business model, we were flexible in terms of implementing new concepts and ideas. At the same time, we recognized the importance of mentoring the expanding number of group leaders. In essence, the group leader (GL) was the key to attracting new and retaining current members.

Our focus after 1995 was to find, groom, and mentor the GL. As the lynchpin of PNG, the GL was continually coached to better performance. Sometimes, we made poor choices in GL's and quietly asked them to step down. We never made these decisions public, so a "retired" GL could remain in the organization without a loss of face.

It was the job of the GL to mentor his or her members. The GL was expected to leverage time by selecting an executive committee (EC) to handle many group functions — planning socials, enlisting new members, etc. By using GL and EC persons to foster our message, we began to see positive attitudes and energy in the group. More and more senior-level people sought out PNG and joined. By the end of the 1990s, PNG was the dominant Southern California player in networking at the highest levels.

From the early days until today, the emphasis at PNG/ProVisors is attracting a trusted advisor with business clients. At the same time, the group makeup included members with overlapping skills, expertise, and services. The basic idea was that, while people might appear to be competitors, almost no one provided the exact same service to the exact same clientele of a similar revenue size. Thus, many of the groups had numerous attorneys, usually each of them with a distinct professional expertise. Even in those cases where people were considered competitive, we often found that they formed alliances and shared leads, rather than acting as direct competitors.

ProVisors thrives today as a one-of-a-kind organization. It is still comprised of many top tier and experienced professionals and emphasizes the willingness of people to share. In fact, the main tenets of ProVisors are the following:

1. While nearly everyone joins with the intent of receiving more business opportunities, the members' foremost

mantra is to reach out to other members and determine how they can help them – the sharing or pay it forward mentality.

2. Members do not sell to the other members. Members are there to be a resource to someone else's clients; thus, the member becomes the access point to business rather than the object of someone's business.

Another critical turning point was the Great Recession starting in late 2007 and early 2008. At that time, the membership ranks were about 1,100. There was also a major shift in how business was conducted – fewer transactions, less reliance on outside professionals, and fee compression for the same or more work. The new normal of being less busy and not overworked set in and has not really changed since 2008. Trusted advisors at all levels in their firm's hierarchy, even those who had previously scorned or just avoided network groups, now needed a place to forge new relationships. Organizations like ProVisors were there to fill the void and prosper as a result. For the next five years, membership more than tripled to 3,500 in June of 2013, when I sold the company.

From time to time in this book, I will refer to my experiences as an owner at ProVisors. It is through this experience, combined with the ideas that have been shared with me, and the books I have read on the topic, that enable me to offer a composite of best networking practices. The primary trait of an authentic networker is the willingness to help other people — the giving part of building relationships. My other proposition for writing this book was to determine if I could answer two networking enigmas: (1) What is the best way to create and maintain your personal network (which usually includes different communities)? (2) Is there a limitation to the number of persons that are contained in your inner core of referrers and resources?

Highlights

1. Learn from my mistake of starting a new business without a sound plan or strong local connections.

2. When faced with failure, take decisive counter action. Working hard and smart are usually a panacea for success.

3. Visualize the results you want by staying in the moment and not being endlessly distracted.

4. Recognize when you have developed or are creating a new service offering or business.

Chapter 2

NETWORK SAUCE

In times like these, it helps to recall that there have always been times like these.
—Paul Harvey

There are still those of you who will never network to any meaningful extent. You may not want or need to network. Some people have their small groups of friends and family, and that is all they need and want. Still others are fearful that networking means people will ask you for things or impose things upon you. In the book *The Startup of You* by Reid Hoffman and Ben Casnocha, the authors discuss the "death" of traditional career paths. No longer can you assume that you will be with one or even two companies for a very long time. Modern society and modern business is in a constant state of flux. There is no such thing as job security.

With that backdrop, the authors of *The Startup of You* suggest that each person should begin to act and think like a startup. Continually reassess your current occupation and future. One excellent means of assessment is to develop a strong and active business community of resources.

You should visualize what may appear to be the impossible.

As you begin to see yourself as a vital part of a larger community or communities, you can then develop the mindset that is required for a life of collaboration. Networking means that you are collaborating on many levels – gathering information, sharing intelligence, finding resources, and gaining new prospects and clients. Also, you are experiencing personal growth and development. At the same time, developing a solid network should also be fun, if it's done properly from a giver's perspective. There are many forms of giving available to each of us. Choose to follow a lifestyle of giving to others in the lynchpin of authentic networking.

> *One example of people helping others was the famous sitcom, Friends. Three young men and three young women shared the same living space. Each was struggling to survive in the real world and found companionship and support within the group as an antidote for everyday pressures.*
>
> *In effect, the group of six was the inner core of a network. They continually met challenges, minor and major, by confiding in one another and serving as emotional buffers and outlets. In some ways, it was difficult for outsiders (e.g. a wife for Ross or a boyfriend for Rachel) to break into the tightly knit group. But at least each one knew he could rely on any of the others for moral and life support.*

Most organized networks are established for professionals or professional service providers. But there are also numerous networks available to executives in corporations. Some of these (e.g. Vistage) are very organized groups of non-competing business executives and business owners who meet monthly. These members serve as each other's board of advisors or board of directors. The meetings are very intense and intended to discuss a variety of business and personal issues that are brought forth by each member in an organized fashion.

In addition to groups such as Vistage, there is the Young Presidents Organization (YPO). This organization is for corporate presidents and owners of their companies that are large enough to meet certain criteria. Again, the YPO community is tightly knit, and a tremendous amount of sharing information and business occurs as a result of this community. Corporate executives who join various industry associations will get together with people in their market or industry to talk about the latest trends, share technology, and build friendships. Many times those friendships will go beyond competing for business. In fact, many of the companies that are sold are sold to primary competitors. What better way to be known and build a relationship than through your local and national industry association.

I have spoken to many corporate executives who resisted joining one of these groups. They just do not feel that vulnerable to things changing. They have not accepted how absolutely powerful those strong relationships and networks are in furthering both one's business and personal growth. Today, more than ever before, it is critical for executives to be involved in various communities. For example, how many times does a person who is not the majority owner of a company, or even a minority owner, find himself out of work? Job mobility is at a heightened pace, with many fungible or interchangeable executive parts. It is this potential or actual vulnerability that should drive the non-owner executive or management person to seek the correspondingly effective community or network.

The most typical excuses for not joining one of these groups are the following:

1. I just do not have the time. I am working at (in) my company ten to twelve hours per day. I just cannot be away from my work or managing my personnel.

2. I am shy and not a group type of person.

3. I really won't learn anything from other people in a group setting, but someone will try to isolate me and sell me something.

4. I have all the resources I need to do my job and do not want to change professionals or vendors.

And the list goes on. There are always as many or more excuses for not joining an organization as there are for joining the same.

Networking History

Many people assume that the birth of networking began with Dale Carnegie in 1937. His first book taught the skills needed to build relationships and create positive outcomes. This book, *How to Win Friends and Influence People*, is still valid today. I presume that ancient cavemen probably formed small "community groups," mainly for protection, sharing ideas on hunting, and generally avoiding dangerous animals.

Perhaps the earliest evidence of collaboration via networking was in Philadelphia in 1725, when Benjamin Franklin set up the Junto for 12, which comprised his most ingenious friends. The purpose of the group meeting was to brainstorm and share ideas. In addition, there were significant discussions of public policy and formulation of responses to public opinion. Franklin was one of the earliest documented persons to harness the talent of others and create the power of shared energy and ideas. Further, in 1765, Franklin set up what might be known as the first formal network called the Club of Honest Whigs. This group was organized in London at the London Coffee House; it is still there today and hosts top-level innovators. Obviously, much has happened since those early days. Numerous forms of organized communities and groups of common interests and values have been established over many years.

Mindset

Your mindset is probably the single most important ingredient in making networking a way of life.

In *The Startup of You*, the authors posit that entrepreneurship is really a lifetime idea and the opposite of laboring. While these concepts are generally attributed to Silicon Valley in California, they are universal. The whole idea is to take intelligent and bold risks and, thereby, achieve the impossible. But it really starts with learning about yourself. Because if you don't understand who you are and how you best interact with other people, you may create relationships that are misdirected or interpreted as "phony." By starting today (and why not today), you are *in essence* an early stage company or early stage person.

If you are not regularly meeting or interacting with other like-minded people, you may want to reassess if you have a safety net community. Much like watching television, you need to change the channel. You should clearly understand that the only way you are going to succeed in the networking game, and it should be a fun game, is by adopting the mindset and intention of a giver.

A consistent, positive attitude will jump-start your networking.

In a recent book by Adam Grant entitled *Give and Take*, the author discussed the differences among givers, matchers, and takers. He defines everyone as part of one of these three, all-encompassing categories. His book provides numerous examples and psychological and sociological studies to confirm his primary points of view.

Obviously, takers are to be avoided. These people give networking a bad rap and a bad name. Do not waste your time with takers, as they will only suck your energy and emotions. Someone once told me that in a crowd, conference, or mixer, you will find people who take the air out of the room (always talking and never listening) or add to the air in the room. Obviously, those that suck the air out of the room are the true takers. There is no amount of time to be devoted to takers.

The matchers are interesting. These are people who give, but believe in the concept of "scoring reciprocity." The principal of reciprocity suggests that for each act of help or sharing toward another human being, there will be some form of nearly equivalent benefit given to you. Matchers are the type of people who really want to keep score and expect some type of quid pro quo for each giving that they provide. Matchers are generally liked and respected, but also treated with some form of skepticism. If you feel that a person is giving you something because they expect some type of reciprocity, you might question their sincerity.

The third type of person, the giver, is bifurcated into two categories. One form of a giver is altruistic, nearly to the extent of giving up everything and his existence to support other people. Grant suggests that these people usually end up at the bottom of the pile or as the least successful people of any type of hierarchy.

Selfless givers are people with high other-interests and low self-interests. They give their time and energy without regard for their own needs, and they pay a price for it. It is an unhealthy focus on others to their own detriment."

The other form of a giver is the ideal person. He is not withholding information; he is willing to share intelligent information even with those who will compete with him. This person is the ultimate giver in terms of providing karma and positive energy. He understands that doing well for others may, and often will, result in good things happening to him. But as important as giving, this person is also open and willing to receive. Thus, this person makes an excellent manager, as well as a loyal employee. This person thinks less about how things will impact him, and more about the common good of his immediate or near-term groups or community affiliations. And, this type of giver is always the most successful in any type of hierarchy or structure. As Grant says,

"If takers are selfish and failed givers are selfless, successful givers are otherish; they care about benefiting others, but they also have ambitious goals for advancing their own interests."

"[The best givers] are able to develop and leverage extraordinarily rich networks. By virtue of the way they interact with other people in their networks, givers create norms that favor adding rather than claiming or trading value, expanding the pie for all involved."

Motivate other people to act like givers. Then they pay it forward.

The movie, Pay it Forward, *is really about otherish, successful givers. A 12-year-old, Trevor McKinney, is given a class project by his teacher, Eugene, to develop a plan of direct action that will change the world. On his way home from school, he befriends a homeless man. Trevor decides he will feed and house the man until he can take care of himself. Trevor develops a plan to "pay it forward" by doing a good deed for three people, each of whom must help three more people, etc. He has created a charitable pyramid scheme.*

The movie contains numerous examples of people committing these otherish acts. For example, a total stranger gives a reporter, Chris, a new Jaguar S-type to replace his recently damaged Ford Mustang. Thus, Chris is very intent on discovering the source of the pay it forward movement. Even Trevor's mother, Arlene, who is an alcoholic, participates by "forwarding" a good deed which gets back to helping her own mother.

The essence or message of this movie is clear. Paying good deeds forward invigorates and enriches your life, as well as each person you "touch".

Many people believe that giving is the healthy choice. It makes us feel good about ourselves to assist other people in furthering their cause.

So now we know what type of mindset or attitude we will adopt. We will eliminate superficiality and, in essence, "get out of ourselves." We will worry less about our own agendas, and listen to the needs of others. This type of authentic networker is interested in improving himself every day. He is always planning ahead as to how he can help others. We are talking about the person who is willing to nurture relationships with friends, family, co-workers, vendors, customers, bosses, and literally any human with whom he comes in contact. This type of action plan creates visibility, credibility and, ultimately, profitability. As the saying goes, "you only get one chance to create a lasting first impression."

Highlights

1. The concept of building or participating in a network community is not new. Various forms or forums have existed since the beginning of civilization.

2. Adapt the right mindset for authentic relationship building, one based on "otherish" giving and paying it forward.

3. There are numerous organizations available to you. Find or create yours and make it work for you.

Chapter 3

NETWORKING MYTHS

The ultimate result of shielding men from the effects of folly is to fill the world with fools.
—Herbert Spencer

During my many years of learning about networking and fostering relationships, I have probably heard every networking myth (i.e., excuse for not putting forth the effort to network). Let me dispel at least some of them.

One More Contact

"I have enough contacts. I do not need to establish one more."

That may well be true for you, so you think. What a burden it is (he said, factiously) to spend the time to connect with another . . . (fill in the blank).

My answer: "You never know." That next person may be your very best connection, friend, business client, etc. Why not be open to at least a phone contact, especially if you trust and respect the person who is giving you the connection? Do you have confidence that the person knows you well enough to make the effort to connect you?

In our business and personal lives, there are obvious direct links, people with whom we can develop meaningful relationships.

So what about the randomness of a next contact? Many network groups have copied the ProVisors troika concept — arranging a meeting of three people outside of a large group meeting. This setting typically enhances the in-depth understanding of another's business and personal life. If a relationship is meant to develop, the troika is a key ingredient.

Now, suppose that one person in the troika is not a direct link, referral source, or resource. Yet, that person has a family connection to a large business, one which really needs your services. The randomness of making connections occurs more often than you might think. Besides, even if there were no direct link or the "random" family business, you can still show up and find out how you can help that person.

<u>Karma paid forward without strings</u> will return to you in some future form; you just don't know how or when.

A "random" business opportunity has occurred for me more than once. At one particular troika, the mortgage broker mentioned that his brother-in-law (B-I-L) had recently acquired a business out of bankruptcy. This B-I-L had prior experience in owning and operating a similar firm, and had already added customers and started to make a profit. In order to grow, the B-I-L's firm needed both debt and equity capital; I mentioned our capability to raise capital. As a result of that information exchange, the mortgage broker arranged for me to meet the B-I-L. By our second meeting, we were retained to raise $15 million for the company.

What would have happened had I not shown up at that troika? Well, nothing, except possibly damage to my reputation for dismissing a pre-set business meeting. Better yet, the "one more contact," though an indirect link, resulted in a sizeable engagement for our firm.

Many people resist that "one more contact" because they feel it is a burden or obligation. How can they befriend someone new, send them business, or serve as a resource to them? You can always find ways to give to someone else. That giving does not have to include a new client.

Not That Function

"I am sure that my attendance at this upcoming mixer will not be worthwhile. Besides, I am very nervous in large groups of people."

How can you decide which function to attend and get maximum returns by meeting the "right" people? First, you must know the type of people who typically attend. Second, understand the agenda for the program/mixer. Will you learn any business intelligence, or is the function simply a "meet and greet?" Third, talk to the organizer of the event about what to expect, key people signed up, and the introductions he will set up for you.

I remember a conference involving medical devices that I attended a few years ago. Initially, I was drawn to attend this function because the speakers and panels were focused on the various stages and forms of capital required in the industry. And, we had valued several medical device companies. To my pleasant surprise, I encountered one of our clients.

For this client, we had valued the intellectual property at various stages of development, primarily to support capital infusions. This equity capital was raised in the startup and venture capital rounds, where we do not participate as an investment banker. The client had grown successfully past the venture stage, and told me they were considering an IPO or outright sale of the business. For some reason, this valuation client was not aware of our investment banking services.

While I had clearly failed to apprise the client of our full range of services, I was fortunate to have attended that function. The aftermath was that we were hired and sold the firm for a significant price.

Attend the function with a few simple goals:

1. Have two to five meaningful conversations; do not "linger" too long with any one person, unless you really have an instant connection. There is always time to arrange a more in-depth, follow-up meeting.

2. Collect business cards and make notes on them for a follow-up meeting. Then make sure you follow-up in a very responsive time frame.

3. Breathe energy into the room; stay upbeat and have fun.

4. Listen for cues as to what excites the other person, what he needs, and how you can help.

5. Confront your fear of large gatherings, since everyone has at least some trepidation. With practice and more frequent attendance, you will get increasingly more comfortable. Then, you will become an introducer or connector. Would you be nervous if these same people were visiting your home?

6. Treat everyone with the same courtesy. At the same time, the 80/20 rule probably applies. That is, spend more of your time (80 percent) on the 20 percent of the people who will likely be your best future links. Disengage politely from the 80 percent after only a brief dialogue.

7. Remain open to sharing something personal about yourself, especially to the 20 percent.

8. LISTEN, LISTEN, and LISTEN by asking open-ended questions that will quickly determine how strong your link may be. For example, if you learn that the other person serves only very small, retail clients and that is not your market, move on to someone else. However, you could introduce that person to another at the function who works in that space. Thus, your reputation as a giver is further enhanced.

9. Stay open to the random person with a "jackpot" solution, referral, client, etc. Remember the expression: You never know.

10. Practice your responses beforehand. Know your unique selling proposition (USP), learn how to deliver it concisely, and blend it into the immediate conversation. The best way is to give a short client example.

11. Control your eager urges. Stay patient throughout the function. Others will definitely "sense" your centered demeanor, and that emanates confidence. Networking is a long-term process with many small, short-term gains.

12. Use the mingling and interaction as part of your personal growth. Even the most experienced professionals and executives are awed by a large gathering of strangers. If you find a "friend" early in the evening, maybe that can settle your nerves. Remember that the purpose of attending is to connect with strangers and further relations with acquaintances who can become future partners.

One of the best ways to counter the fear of a large room of strangers is to assume <u>you are</u> and <u>act like</u> the host of the function.

NETWORKING MYTHS

I Am Not Memorable

"I am not physically imposing, so no one will remember me. How do I make a good impression?"

The very best way to be memorable upon first meeting someone is to exhibit a sense of humor and interest in him. Being noteworthy to others is largely dependent on you being yourself. To improve the "positive you," acknowledge how and when you were the most sincere. Bottle that attitude. When you meet new people and maintain a positive mental attitude, you are attractive. You are someone others are drawn to and want to get to know.

Be sincerely interested in what others say and do.
Also, be interesting, so others are drawn to you.

Showing passion for your work helps others better relate to you and your expertise. Your personal beliefs in helping others and being a trusted advisor are central to others impression of you. Become the hub of the wheel, not the spoke.

You are a central focal point when you deliver the information or resources someone needs. You are the casting director for your own play, and show the characters how to interact for their benefit.

Each person is memorable. Some just do not know how to show it. Have you ever stood in a room full of people and noticed how many people approach you? Or, how many approach and group around specific people? It's what I call the Centers of Influence (COI). If you want the respect and attention, figure out the best way to become a well-known COI. Obviously, this type of attraction is usually earned over a period of time. Your job is to become a COI in as short a time frame as possible. Be the IT factor, and reach out to other IT people. That is the best way to accelerate your business and social connections.

As the initial creator of ProVisors, I am personally known by many of the members. That alone was not enough for me. I also attended most of the group meetings and major functions (lunches, dinners, and mixers). I was the "face" of ProVisors and often took the opportunity to explain the mission and benefits of the organization. On top of this, I really enjoy meeting new people and determining how I can share or give to them. I am always connecting professionals and business executives/owners with direct links to further their business or personal growth and objectives. That is who I am, and it makes me a COI. If you want to be a COI, you need to adopt a strategy for doing so. If being a COI is a natural role for you and it is part of your business game plan, start now on a track that gets you there.

Don't Like Small Talk

"I hate small talk. It is tedious and boring. So how do I avoid it?"

Most people want more than chitchat or small talk. But some of it is necessary as a way of greeting others or not being awkward in social settings. Small talk can lead to deeper conversations, or you can direct it there. The art of segue is probably the most underrated personal communication skill. Often, humor is a good way to switch topics or focus in a conversation. Use it if it is a natural part of your personality. False or stilted attempts at humor are worse than not invoking humor. Be true to yourself. The best way to improve your communication style and impact is to get help from a professional coach who can personally train you.

I do not consider myself the most inspirational or ideal public speaker. I am much better, and more comfortable, leading a group setting, whereby I can interact with others and respond to their dialogue and comments. Prior to presenting to an audience, I have the natural or normal trepidations. I find it interesting that some people are perfectly comfortable giving a prepared speech, but very insecure in a first one-on-one meeting. Find your level of comfort and work to improve it. It may be the difference between being average or successful. Like most speakers/presenters, the more I practice my delivery, the better the outcome. In *Own the*

Room, the authors explain that good preparation does not mean memorization or reading from a teleprompter. It does mean knowing your materials, capturing a tone and rhythm, and then sharing yourself with your audience. To that end, I enjoy presenting at least a part of me in every talk.

Networking is Beneath Me

"I am a senior professional/executive. I will likely never meet or connect with someone on my level."

Maybe not, but why preclude the possibility of making that connection? EVERY HUMAN NEEDS AND WANTS TO BE CONNECTED TO A LIKE-MINDED COMMUNITY. I think even Henry David Thoreau left the wilderness to return to some societal connections — and, maybe to get his writings published!

The movie, *It's a Wonderful Life*, clearly depicts how building a great community may be life-altering.

> *If George Bailey (James Stewart in* It's a Wonderful Life*) had this attitude, his life would have been ruined. The story begins with George about to commit suicide. His companion is an angel-trainee named Clarence, who will get his wings if he can save George from his suicide mission.*
>
> *The film flashes back in time to explain George's predicament. George was planning to leave his town of Bedford Falls, headed to Europe before matriculating at college. His father, who owns a Savings & Loan (S&L) company, dies suddenly. George aborts his grand plans and settles in to operate the S&L. The evil protagonist is Mr. Potter, owner of the town bank.*
>
> *One day, George's uncle loses a substantial cash deposit on the way to Potter's bank. Potter finds the bag*

of cash, but does not tell George. George is panic-stricken, but promises to repay the lost deposit to Potter (now in the form of a loan to George's S&L). To prevent a run of his S&L, George calls a meeting of all town people who are his customers. His friends and customers agree to leave their money in his S&L. However, Potter calls the loan and threatens to take over the S&L.

Thus, George goes into suicide mode. Clarence stops him, and then shows him how badly the town of Bedford Falls would have become without George. Fortified by Clarence's dire depiction of a ruined city, George goes home to painfully tell his wife and family of his impending financial ruin. Waiting for George at his house are the good citizens of Bedford Falls. They have pooled their money to repay the Potter loan, saving George and the S&L.

The obvious moral is that George was remarkably well-liked, respected, and networked. His community of friends "paid" him the highest accolade by saving him from his worst nightmare – shame and suicide.

Each of us knows or knows of high-powered, well-connected people who were born into privilege. Some have been mentored by industry or political power brokers. Some have just insinuated themselves into and among high-level connections that provide a continual flow of capital, opportunity, and career moves, or access to the right resources. Still, others have parlayed family members or legacies, or offspring of the wealthy, into situational success. At the same time, the above examples of apparent access to money, power, or higher levels of achievers were really accomplished by connections to the "right" people. The central tenet is still about relationships. My supposition is that, at some time, everyone needs help from someone. Starting with clubs or sports as kids, people begin to belong and make friends. There are numerous types of loose or well-structured organizations that proliferate in our personal and business lives.

Margaret Wheatley, a consultant who studies organization behavior, concluded:

> *Relationships are all there is. Everything in the universe only exists because it is in relationship to everything else. Nothing exists in isolation. We have to stop pretending we are individuals that can go it alone.*

Author Mitch Albom of *Tuesdays with Morrie*, stated: "Build a little community of those you love and who love you. We all need that core community of love. Without it we are either lost, adrift, or without purpose and meaning in our life." The stronger that love corridor, the easier it is to put yourself out there, and fail.

As a junior and senior in high school, I had been told by a local business person that I would receive a full scholarship to The University of Michigan for basketball and baseball. Looking back on that time, I was never in direct contact with the head coach for either sport. I was relying on the word of a local "scout," since I did not understand the recruiting process. How naïve of me, or maybe how relatively unimportant I was to Michigan.

The only other school to which I applied (and was accepted) was Dartmouth. My high school football coach and athletic director talked briefly to the Dartmouth coach when he visited our high school. Though I played football in high school, I was not planning to play that sport in college. He knew I also played basketball and baseball, so he emphasized the academics and the fact that I could play these other sports.

I made a recruiting trip to Dartmouth with my parents. What a stark difference in athletic emphasis and facilities between the two schools (Big 10 and Ivy League), to say nothing of the talent disparity.

When I was sent a letter by Michigan's basketball coach and asked to walk-on (not granted an athletic scholarship), I was extremely disappointed. My entire life's focus and athletic dreams had included playing at The University of Michigan. The Ivy League, which included Dartmouth, did not (nor does it today) provide athletic scholarships. I was granted a student loan to Dartmouth, which allowed me to matriculate there.

How did that setback or failure turn out? It wasn't all bad. I played both sports at Dartmouth, earning All-Ivy honors for three years in basketball. And, I got an excellent education.

Whenever I have been forced to take a new or different path, I have made it work; ¾ but not without "falling down" on occasion, or struggling financially. Remember why I created the networking organization. I was forced to figure out how to survive and build a business, unlike any of my other past experiences.

Along the way to success in my professional business life, I built a framework for untold numbers of network members to amass small to sizeable fortunes.

Too Young To Network

"I lack the experience to talk with or share anything with most of the people I meet. They will not pay attention to me."

As PNG was growing slowly throughout the 1990s, there was some thought to attracting younger professionals with great upside potential. But the older pros were resistant, wanting to keep the community serving their needs. The strong, younger ones persisted; a few even became group leaders. It is at this level, group leader (GL), that you are accorded an elevated level of respect. You not only decide which people can join your group, but how the meetings will be conducted (given the basic framework within which all groups operate).

ProVisors has adapted well to accommodate all types of professionals, including many in their 30s and even late 20s. The pressure is on these younger members to deliver ideas, connections, and referrals. So long as they share first or pay it forward, age differentials disappear. In fact, many groups target younger people, attempting to create a more energetic, fresh communication.

Obviously, you are never too young or too old to begin networking. Parents should encourage their children to build relationships and friendships very early and often in life. As you find your passion/occupational path, you may want to reach out to these prior connections. When I left ADLV in 1987, I had no more than six names in my Rolodex. From that paltry number, I contacted a senior person at the accounting firm KPMG. He was kind enough to hire us for one of his clients, a valuation engagement that was large enough to carry our firm for several months. But *no one* should be that desperate. I was very fortunate for the great business jumpstart. I will never be in that dire position again, nor should you.

What else can you do as a younger professional or executive? Most importantly, get out of the office. Even if your primary job is not to generate business, will anyone in your firm turn down a good assignment that you originate?

Here are a few ways to start branding yourself, even as a younger person:

1. True passion trumps all. Express what you are passionate about, though in a matter-of-fact way. We are drawn to the person who can articulate why he enjoys the work. That makes us more curious about how we can help.

2. Give, Give, Give. Find out what is meaningful to others, even seasoned veterans (old folks!), and reach out to offer *something*. Giving to others triggers the "human guilt switch." When we receive something of value that we did not solicit,

our brain receptors are wired to record that occurrence in our long-term memory. Those key introductions you make that result in a new friendship or business relationship are especially unforgettable.

3. How many actors who "suddenly" become famous did not toil in some anonymity for years? Very few.

4. Arrange meetings with your elders and learn from them. Find out how they forged a career and what you can do to best present yourself. People want to help eager younger people. So ask.

5. Organize a mastermind group of younger professionals. Develop a chemistry with those in the group most likely to be resources and referrers for you and your clients. While you should always be open to receiving, the best way to be a "receiver" is to start by being the giving "quarterback."

6. Start your own firm or move to one where your value is better appreciated. There may be a time when you are ready to go on your own, or with a few partners. Choose those partners wisely, with clearly defined roles, compensation, lifestyle, decision-making procedures, etc. The ultimate arbiter of a successful venture is the trust in one another. If complete trust is lacking, wait for a better opportunity.

I have experienced good to awful (painful, in fact) "partnerships." Spanning my business career, I have started five firms, bought one, and sold four. That leaves two companies that I continue to own and operate. Most of us need to work cooperatively with others, within our firm or outside. The least successful of my ventures were those where my reliance on others to deliver their promised output did not match my expectations.

*Success is a building process. Few good
things happen overnight.*

Network Momentum

"In order to be an effective networker, you need to maintain a certain momentum. I will have too many lapses from doing real or billable work, or my lack of ongoing participation will be negative."

While sporadic participation is not the best course of action, no participation is worse. We respond to someone's demeanor and immediacy, and their willingness to listen and relate to our conversation. Stay in the moment and do not worry about your lack of "momentum."

It is true that momentum overcomes inertia (a body at rest tends to remain at rest unless a force creates some motion). Just the act of doing something periodically or every once in a while is a form of momentum. To achieve some results, this activity must at least be consistent and thoughtful. It need not be continual, nor should it overwhelm you or cause burnout. Stay fresh by changing your routine or going to different types of functions on occasion. If you are truly bored, that "feeling" will be on display.

Individual vs. Village

"I need others to go with me, sort of a buddy or village approach."

If it helps to attend with a friend or a group, that is fine. Do whatever works to actually attend the function. Make each appearance part of a planned approach.

At the most basic level, how you show up is what people remember about you. The ability to network may be a learned activity for some, so seeing your buddy in action may be useful. Understand your uneasy feelings and how to move past them. Before you give an elevator pitch, you may need to settle yourself. Make sure your voice is lubricated and your breathing is even. If you focus on your breathing and not your message, you will likely deliver a confident introduction.

Practice, practice, practice your brief message, as well as any client stories. Then, you can insert the message and stories at appropriate times. Remember to listen first and relate to what is said to you directly.

Also, introduce yourself to a wallflower. He is probably shyer than you. The wallflowers are often technically savvy, but lack confidence to open the conversation.

Easy to Burnout

"If I go too often to any function, I will display fatigue or burnout."

You might. Most functions take on familiar routines. So it is not uncommon to become blasé or show boredom.

Mix up your routine. It may help to attach to people you know, at least at first. As you settle in, be bolder and talk to a stranger or two. Sometimes you can use humor, a clothing accessory, or other impersonal thing to ignite the discourse. That often reduces the tension, especially if the strangers are in a group discussion.

I Don't Follow Plans

"I do not follow a plan. So why make one, especially for networking?"

A well-developed plan is only as good as your delivery against it. But crafting a plan will usually condition you to follow some routine or strategy. A networking plan reinforces that you need to "keep on, keeping on;" it pushes you beyond just busying yourself in real work and neglecting the networking.

Preparation is the pre-cursor of the
results you seek and deserve.

When you plan ahead for several months to a year, you set your mind to a course of action. You can always vary the plan to cover current exigencies. But the plan becomes part of a focused mindset. Most of us like to fulfill at least parts of our plan, so we "see" and experience small successes. Many small achievements often lead to bigger results.

What If I Fail?

"If I do not get involved, I cannot fail."

This answer is too obvious. If you never take action, you are by definition failing to achieve. You also know that failure is only a temporary course correction on your highway of success.

Think of networking as being wrapped in a blanket. The people you encounter are the blanket. Let them engulf and warm you. They will if you show genuine interest in them. Value them and produce value by giving. And repeat. And repeat. And repeat. The only failures are the takers or those who do not show up.

Busy is Not Necessarily Good

"I do not like non-productive work time. Why would I subject myself to just "busy" networking?"

Focused busy time is good. Being present is *usually* better than not attending. Why? There are several reasons:

1. A random connection may result in a new engagement.

2. Conversation begets more conversation, out of which newer perspectives are enunciated and client needs are identified.

3. Good busy means you have planned to attend the best events/meetings.

4. You cannot afford to be out-of-touch for long periods, or even short ones. Once people forget about you, you are forgotten.

5. When seeing you gives the other party a "warm fuzzy" feeling, you will become top of mind for the next referral.

Refuse to Sell

"To me, networking is just a fancy name for selling. And I refuse to be a salesperson."

Okay. I get it. However, no matter who you are or what you do, you probably need to "sell yourself" to someone, if only your boss. How can you expect to advance, succeed, or just better your place in life unless someone in a position of power or influence will support you? Even though one may think he won't or can't "sell," the act of selling does not need to be castigated or thought of as something negative. Selling does not connote that the receiving or buying party has been conned. It only means that someone has sold something to someone who has purchased. In fact, the best salespeople do not "hard sell," since almost no buyer will allow that approach. The best ones merely connect with the emotional pain/need of the buying party, and the sale happens as a result.

If your impression is that networking is actually the same thing as the dreaded "selling," I understand your avoidance. However, networking is what you make it, since you control the time spent, approach to making connections, and the outcomes. No one likes being sold, so the most authentic style precludes direct selling/pitching. And the "sellers" or "takers" are decidedly shunned. I suggest you change your headset and at least be open to meeting contacts that can play an important role in your life.

No Need to Network

"I have no desire or need to network. I am busy enough."

I wonder how many people who said that before 2008 can say the same thing today. For the vast majority of professionals I know, there is a new normal of activity. The hectic pace of work from 2003 to 2008 has been replaced with periods of less demanding workloads, punctuated only periodically by high activity reminiscent of that five-year period.

I also think that those who go to lengths to avoid meeting with others outside their firm are just more reclusive. If you never have to worry about your next engagement or where you need to spend your work time, you are blessed.

However, you are also missing the opportunities to learn vital and current information from others, often useful to your clients and/or other executives in your firm. And, you are not taking advantage of the personal growth which occurs each time you interact and refine your message or brand. These interactions are constructive in terms of furthering your career and your connections with key persons in your "space," industry, or the community at large. Reframe an old adage: Never turn away a potential gift-horse in the anticipation that it is a Trojan horse.

How Can I Trust

"Even if I meet someone at a networking function, how can I trust the person enough to help or send him or her business?"

The simple answer is that trust is a long-term process "under construction." It rarely happens quickly. If you want to *not* make a referral to or share any information with another person, you can blame it on lack of trust.

Again, there is no shortcut to creating trust. It is probably the ultimate bond. Once broken, it is typically irreparable. But let's focus on how to build it. Your own reputation is a start. So long as that is beyond reproach, there is a foundation for trust. From that basis, your consistent and responsible actions move you along the reliance spectrum. I also believe that confidence in one another is partly hinged on working together on a project. It is also formed from a confluence of things, not the least of which is getting positive feedback from others, solicited or otherwise.

My ultimate example of a trusting relationship is my 35 year marriage to my wife. A second favorite is the ongoing business and friendship with my partner, Brad Cashion. In 1992, Brad was invited to meet with the partners of The Mentor Group. I had not met him before. Since we were a small firm at the time, each potential addition to the professional staff was a critical decision. At the time, Brad was in his late 20s, with less than three years actual experience in financial valuation. Offsetting this was his poise, openness, and unusual understanding of our business. While I perceived that he was very smart and eager to succeed, the thing that resonated the most with me was his openness and trustworthiness. To this day, Brad and I are very close working partners and friends.

I believe you are much better off leveraging relationships of trust. At least you need to know when you can rely on another's integrity to get a job done. "Trust but verify" is a much more positive way to live than the alternative of not placing any faith in even a few people.

People Take Advantage

"People are fake. They always end up taking advantage of me and others."

Unfortunately, many people are not who they purport to be. I suggest that you take the opportunity to make strong connections that can evolve into business relationships. Not everyone becomes a business connection or friend; on the other hand, some will. Remember, your capacity and capability to stay in front of and close to many people is limited. Distinguish the givers from all others.

Risk Losing the Client

"The only thing that can happen if I refer someone is a bad outcome. So why network if I won't refer anyone."

The above is a tough attitude to counter. To this person, the risk far exceeds any possible reward. That reward, which would be appreciation from a referral source and the client, is not worth the risk.

Another way to position your thinking is the following: Is the client, or person to whom I am referring, better off with my choice(s) or a random choice not from me? Random may seem a safer bet, but does it really help the receiving person? Only you can answer these questions.

The true purpose of authentic networking is to vet who you know into trusting advisors — people you can really rely on to deliver what you want, when you want. And, hopefully you never even think about the referral consequence of losing a client. The best hand-off of a referral is to clearly position the person(s) with a client, explaining what you know and appreciate about that person.

Reluctant to Follow-up

"I am reluctant to chase down or make an appointment with a newer contact. It will never result in a business relationship."

Whoa. You need a "Five-Hour Confidence Boost." That myth or excuse is pretty lame, or even broken. I think your inner critic is overmatching your inner confidence builder (champion). When that happens, you are self-defeating. Your business development initiative is shutdown. Shake it off. Never say never. Or, in the words of Winston Churchill, "Never, never give up."

My Work Sells Itself

"The quality of my work sells itself. I will always have clients come to me based on my professionalism."

They may, and they may not. Clients are more fickle these days, requiring more attention, positive reinforcement, and some fee concessions. Since 2008, in most professions there is increased scrutiny of our services and fees. The downward fee compression is particularly vexing, since the financial, accounting, and tax standards for quality and work product are much more stringent.

The best way to ensure a steady stream of prospects and repeat clients is to perform to the utmost of your ability and standards. That is axiomatic. However, without highlighting the benefits of our work, some clients will never know how well we performed. You can be a major "megaphone" for other professionals, simply by reinforcing the high quality of their service to common clients, prospects, or referral sources. A compliment from a respected person usually carries more clout than self-proclamation.

One story that particularly stands out involved a referred client and their tax attorney. We were referred to the client by this attorney, a very professional but unassuming person. The potential engagement involved the valuation of patents and proprietary, unpatented technology. The valuation was needed to support a transaction involving the patents that were being licensed to a competitor for their exclusive use. Thus, our assignment was to value this IP and develop arm's-length royalty (licensing) rates. At the first meeting with the Chief Financial Officer (CFO) of the prospect, he asked me how I knew the tax attorney. I replied that we had worked together on a few mutual clients. And, I added that the client was fortunate to work with such a creative professional and exemplary person. Somewhat taken aback, the client smiled, and thanked me for my opinion. The CFO admitted that he thought his attorney was excellent, but he was also glad to hear that confirmation from another professional.

While we may think others know how professional their trusted advisors are, they often do not. When true and appropriate, providing a sincere endorsement, even of an existing advisor, is the ultimate form of payback and reciprocity.

Highlights

1. Understand your excuses (myths) for not networking, and find a way to get beyond these roadblocks.

2. Even if you do not belong to a formal community, you probably have an informal way to pursue connections. Why not arrange for your inner circle of contacts to meet together on a regular basis?

3. Networking takes time and effort. Develop a plan to devote the proper energy to building or participating in a community of your choice.

Chapter 4

THE MAGIC NUMBERS

You can never step into the same river twice, for new waters are always flowing on to you.
—Heraclitus

When I decided to write this book, there was one central question I wanted to answer: Is there a limitation on the size of one's network? In other words, are there optimum and maximum numbers of people with whom you can maintain meaningful relations? As I am defining a network, it can and should encompass all types of people with whom you have some degree of connectivity. Examples include friends, family, co-workers, country club members, and members of your church, synagogue, book club, workout group, etc.

The main reason to seek a pure number, or a quantification of one's network, is to ascertain whether what we are doing is maximizing our connections or overtaxing our abilities.

Major considerations or questions surrounding the quantification of our networks are the following:

1. Do you need or want to connect people, such as a synagogue or church member, to various communities in your primary business network? Is that a practical or desirable goal?

2. Do you know who is already in your various networks?

3. Are there some natural limitations on the number of people with whom you can maintain meaningful ties? What are those numbers and how does that affect your networking program?

4. How do I define my core groups? The A Core would be my innermost circle; the B Core would include less substantial relationships than the A Core. Each person has a different definition as to whom and how many are in his or her A, B, and C Core groups.

Network Cores

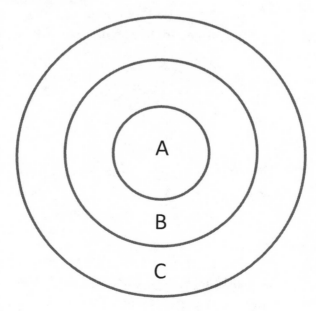

There are no easy or simple answers to organizing and maintaining a viable network. It is up to each individual to define and determine what those core groups consist of and how people may flow in and out of the various concentric circles. Obviously, the C Core constitutes the many people with whom we want to maintain some contact, if only via an occasional email.

There may be various types of persons in your A Core. Once you get past the friends and family individuals, are there business connections that provide you new contacts, referrals, intelligence, or new resources? What type of giving do they offer or do you offer them? The best contact management systems allow you to input numerous descriptors to separate your database into logical groupings. At a minimum, you will want to sort them by profession, specialty, referral source, resource, community, etc. It is important to make these distinctions, especially within your A and B Cores. Until you know how others fit into your network, it is difficult to organize a plan to properly maintain connectivity.

Dunbar's Number

I am not the first or the last person to ask these types of questions, particularly the quality and quantity of network contacts. In 1992, an evolutionary anthropologist named Robin Dunbar authored a study titled *How Many Friends Does One Person Need?* Dunbar is the director of the Institute of Cognitive and Evolutionary Anthropology at Oxford University. It is also worth noting that the year in which he conducted his analysis was prior to the Internet being widely available for use.

Dunbar found a general relationship between the size of the brain and size of the social group.

The thesis of Dunbar's study was that we have no choice about the way we behave. Our social behavior is rooted in our biology, such that we are programmed to follow the rules of playing the game of life. Within this game, there are different social circles and layers, but he suggested a natural grouping of about 150 people. This idea has become known as Dunbar's Number. This number represents the people that you can have relationships with at any given time, based upon trust and obligation. This is the group that requires a personal history, not just names and faces in the database. This number does not represent the many people that you might know, or come in contact with in a lifetime. However, it does identify the number of people that you can maintain stable, social relationships with on a regular basis. Now that we are in the age of advanced and rapidly changing technology, often termed "social media," is Dunbar's Number at all meaningful?

Dunbar's Number

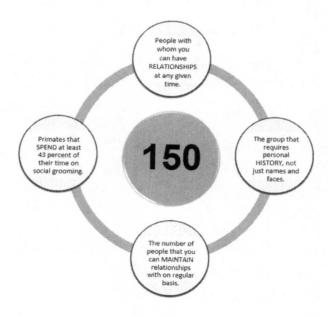

Another aspect of Dunbar's Number (and his regression analysis) was that the community of 150 primates would be required to spend at least 43 percent of its time on social grooming. Therefore, Dunbar suggested that 150 was an upper number rather than an optimum. Another corollary to this number is the amount of employees at which an entrepreneurial company loses its individual spirit and flare, and becomes a more structured organization. Dunbar found corroborative evidence from studies of both corporations and hunter-gather tribes. For example, Hutterite Farming Communities had a rule that they must split into a new community when the current one reached 150 people. This was based on the rationale that it was impossible to control morals and behaviors through peer pressure beyond that point. Furthermore, as towns and cities evolved in the medieval and post-medieval days, the number of 150 was generally accepted as the point at which members of that town or unit would split off to form new units or communities.

Even with today's Internet, is being well-connected
to 150 people realistic? Only if you make it so.

In a piece entitled *Collaboration*, author Morton Hansen discussed the fact that Dunbar's Number is completely irrelevant in today's world of social media and networking online. He also stated that weak relationships (or those outside of our A and B Cores, to use my terms) are not only important but necessary. These outlier relationships enable us to extend our current circles. It is very typical that within our A Core, one friend will know many of the same people and the things that we know. At the same time, our ties in the B and C Cores may be the most critical to our thinking. Because they are not so intractably linked with us, they may provide a new base of information, as well as fresh, sometimes positively disruptive ideas.

Based upon numerous conversations with colleagues over the years, I know that each person has his or her own Dunbar's Number. Many people think their A Core or number is between five and twenty people. Personally, I believe that number is extremely low. In my two businesses, valuations and investment banking, my primary responsibilities are focused on connecting with referral sources and resources to develop prospects into clients; being available to respond to specific client issues; and managing and directing staff to achieve more and better results. Thus, my thinking on the "magic number" may be skewed, compared to a corporate executive who does little networking outside of his company.

Most corporate executives are isolated, relying upon a very small handful of two to five trusted advisors at any one point in time. This occurs principally because, as executives have elevated their position to managing numerous people, they are much more inwardly focused than outwardly. They are also cloistered in a bubble, so to speak. In that state, they avoid people from the outside trying to sell or get something from them. They also fall into the dangerous trap that they never have to worry about their work life or work position, that somehow they are rather secure or insular in their current responsibilities, company, or circles of friends and influencers. Thus, it is often very difficult to convince corporate executives to venture outside of their narrow perimeter or business world. Think about this: If you do not own a company or at least have majority control of a company (or have a very complicit partner), you are always vulnerable to being fired or displaced. Today, executives who do not keep expanding their horizons and networks may become endangered species.

As a case in point, there is a vivid example of a "C-suite" person who was rather isolated (not "naked," but close) as a chief financial officer. A few years ago, Michael and I were connected by a referral source shortly after his firm acquired another company. Michael hired us to value all of the tangible and intangible assets. As I got to know Michael, I appreciated his congenial style and expertise. One day, Michael called and said that he had been fired because his company was downsizing and potentially going out of business. I asked Michael to meet with me. While he had not decided his next career move, I suggested that he incorporate a business to serve as a part-time chief financial officer (CFO). In other words, he would offer his services on a short-term or interim basis for companies who could not or would not afford a full-time CFO. In addition, I asked Michael to join the ProVisors group where I was the group leader. For the next two years, since he was very competent and collaborative, Michael did well as an interim CFO. Then, the inevitable happened. He was lured back into a full-time position with a fast growing company.

You might have guessed what happened next. Michael told me that he was leaving ProVisors. Since he did not have a strong "other" community to rely on, I nearly pleaded with him to stay in the community where he was welcomed. I realized that his new corporate position might limit his time to participate in ProVisors, unless he spent a few hours each week away from his place of business. I knew that he was giving up some of his A Core connections. As is true with most people who are corporate types, Michael felt that this new position would last for a long time. Since Michael left ProVisors, I have had very little contact with him. I understand what he thought at the time — he no longer needed to network. I felt he was making a mistake in giving up tightly knit relationships which he had nurtured and developed. Unfortunately, this story is all too endemic of most people who work in Corporate America.

Blaine's Number

I have given a lot of thought to the number of people that one can maintain in his network today, especially a professional service provider. My belief is that a substantial C Core is between 2,000 and 3,000 people. To many, that may seem like a gigantic number. However, if you have focused on maintaining and cultivating relationships and alliances, you can and will find a way to develop that size of database. This does not mean you will interact with these people on a regular basis. Rather, these contacts will be mostly email or LinkedIn connections, and not consistently available to you. While there is no specific timetable for making these connections, you might consider quarterly email blasts as an effective way to reach this core.

How would I define my A Core? At the outset of writing this book, it was one of my stated goals that I would discover my Dunbar Number for the A Core, which I now refer to as Blaine's Number. Deeply involved in ProVisors for nearly three decades, I continually analyzed how the organization could implement better member benefits. However, while I have connected with thousands of people during this time, I had never analyzed my extensive database to quantify my cores — until I wrote this book.

*For maximum efficiency, you should analyze
at least your A and B cores often.*

The results of my analysis were the following: My A Core is about 110, while the B Core is an additional 400 plus. I believe the exercise of placing contacts into each group will clearly define my most important relationships, or those I want to re-create or improve. I plan to meet with most of my A Core twice a year, and some of them three to four times a year. I also know that the conversations may well broach the subject as to whether we are in each other's A Core. Rather than leaving this potentially meaningful connection to chance, I will focus on the "how" and "why" we should be relevant to one another. You can only expect to receive honest feedback about the importance of your relationship when you ask. Since my A Core is large, I know it is not possible to give each person a prospective new client in a year. The emphasis is not on direct reciprocity; although, I hope that happens. The focus is how I can help the other person at the time I meet with him, or even in between sessions. This focus will make me think of the A Core people as much as possible. It will also help me decide if my initial selections need to be changed (e.g. an A becomes a B or a new A emerges). In any event, I am practicing what I preach.

If I know how I want to interact with my A's, what should I consider for connecting with my B's? And how likely is it that I can have any meaningful contact with this group of people? Most often, a B person is a newer acquaintance or one with whom I have not closely participated (e.g. a client matter). My plan includes periodically meeting with the B Core people, especially when they have reached out to share something with me – a new contact, a prospective client, etc. Also, I always remain open to circumstances that place me in close proximity to or serving on a team of other trusted advisors, which may include B's.

I had a recent discussion with another professional who reflected on how he uses LinkedIn. Whenever he is asked to link to a new person, he pulls down that person's profile. If that person has more than 500 viable connections on LinkedIn, he always chooses to exclude them from a connection with himself. His theory is if a person has more than 500 connections, he will be lost in the law of large numbers. He believes that he is very unlikely to establish any type of meaningful relationship to that person. My view point is somewhat opposite. I think if a person has more than 500 connections, I want to link to them. Why? My obvious reason is that if I need a particular type of connection to someone who may be difficult to directly access, that person with 500 or more connections on LinkedIn could be part of an answer to the puzzle, or at least move me along the chain toward an introduction to the person I am seeking to meet via the Internet. In addition, often the most valuable network is made up of people who are high-energy, high-quantity, and high-quality connectors. Why not be closely connected to a person who is a Center of Influence connector? This does not mean that you will become best friends or put that person in your A Core, but you might.

Get Out of Yourself

The same concept of being closely allied or connected to a well-known connector is part of my philosophy. Usually, the primary and only thing which impedes us from a higher-level of happiness and/or success is our self.

We are often our own worst enemy. I have often suggested to other people that one of the ways to move into a nearly Zen-like status is to "get out of yourself" when dealing with other people. Do not try to insert your agenda into the conversation. Rather, listen for the other person's needs. The most understandable format for that state of being is that we put aside our own thoughts, opinions, and agenda, and merely exist in a connected state with that other person or persons. That is generally the best state in which to be, since it allows us to be an open and interested listener. This does not mean that we can't participate and share our ideas or passions about a particular issue or topic. However, it does mean that we have removed or pushed aside the baggage in our brain and are much less concerned with impressing the other person or pushing our agenda. This Zen-like position allows us to clearly understand how we can help the other person at that moment. It also allows us to give openly without worrying about what is in it for us.

*As a permanent or disruptive beta, we should
be able to increase the peripheral vision
of what is often our narrow lens.*

In *The Startup of You*, the authors refer to a concept called "living in permanent beta." Essentially this is the act of always testing our ideas and how we relate to people through our unique lens. I have applied this mindset and found it very productive. However, we can only achieve this state of being if we get out of ourselves and our own way, and keep an open mind in our interactions with others.

What's in Your Core(s)?

As a young partner in his firm, corporate attorney Joel Berman had almost no clients. With the help of a business coach, he began to realize that, among other things, participating in networking groups provided a pathway to building a book of business. Twenty years later, he became one of the top rainmakers in his firm and finds many opportunities to refer business outside his firm. Over the years, he has developed an A Core membership consisting of about 50 people. His stated approach is to meet with each of these people quarterly. Obviously, he is continually meeting with trusted advisors and potential clients. He also participates in eight monthly network organizations or groups, three of which are part of ProVisors. Some of the other groups are not part of an organized system. But in most of these, he is either the leader or has been instrumental in placing members into the group.

Joel uses speaking engagements to connect with larger groups, especially accountants. His presentations focus on lessons he has learned about the absolute power of authentic networking.

In addition to his speaking engagements, Joel schedules numerous one-on-one sessions, usually over breakfast or lunch, to reconnect often with his A Core and, when possible, other referral sources. He also attends many troikas. Since he is involved in eight groups. Joel says that he practices law in between meals.

Upon meeting someone, Joel usually asks one or more of the following five open-ended questions:

1. Who are your best clients?

2. Who are your best referral sources?

3. How do you market yourself?

4. What is your biggest challenge in business today?

5. Where do you want to be in five years?

Joel contends that by focusing on these questions, he can find ways to help anyone. And, through the dialogue that follows, he quickly determines how much he can trust this person.

Reflect on what Joel is doing. He wants to learn the latest about someone's life or business, which is essential to any relationship. Never assume one's life is static, and always be open to new information. It formulates the current basis for giving. While the apparent opposite of giving is getting, the two are closely allied. To allow others to give to you is an act of honoring their giving. It elevates your connections, while stimulating the next round or incidence of your giving back. Few relish the "guilt" of owing you something.

Joel and I discussed two different ways to build a network:

- Shallow and broad. Have many contacts in various categories of professionals. Some might say "shallow" connotes that one has too many contacts, with less ability to know them on a deeper level.

- Narrow and deep. Converse more with a few A Core people you meet on a regular basis, with each relationship being intensely personal. Tight bonds and friendships are the result, but potential opportunities may be foregone simply because you close off new entrants.

Joel and I think the best way is a combination of the two above. While narrow and deep can be very powerful, it can leave you vulnerable. Do you stop adding key allies when you cannot give each of them referrals? And if they refer to you, why is there a criterion that requires you to reciprocate? Perhaps that is your mindset, but a true A Core person will not assume that life requires "balancing the books" quarterly or even yearly. What if someone in your narrow core moves out of the area, leaves the profession, or is incapacitated for a long period? These changes, which can happen to anyone, could greatly impair your core referrals or resources.

Another aspect of your concentric circles (cores) is whether they favor referrers or resources. The ideal is a matching or an inner core of people who will refer you and whomever you can refer. Yet, the world is not perfect. Populate your cores with those people you relate to best. That friendship will ultimately lead to finding ways to help one another. Likely, you need more than one relationship with each type of trusted advisor you consider a resource. If the number of "types" to whom you refer or work closely with is between 10 and15, then your A Core could easily be between 30 and 40 people. Keep in perspective the fact that matching or close matching almost never occurs. So while you need not keep "score," keep a record of referrals you make and receive.

Young Professionals

I often talk with groups of professionals, graduate students, or executives about the relevance of making lasting connections. Recently, I was asked to address a group of younger attorneys on the power of a having solid network. The challenge of building a network is unlike anything you learn in college or graduate school. Here are a few of the harsh realities that young lawyers and accountants face in mid-size to large firms:

1. You are well compensated to stay in the office and work 12 to 15 hours a day, including at least one weekend day.

2. For at least two to four years, your focus is completely on servicing the partners in your firm and their clients. Your interaction with clients, except in a few instances, may be limited.

3. At the four- to five-year mark, you know whether you are on the partner track. And the conversation turns to how soon the firm expects you to bring in clients. Wow, why didn't someone tell you earlier in your career to start building a network? And why didn't the firm let you out of the office to network?

The world of collaboration is completely open to younger people who are intent on digging for oysters to find the pearls.

Faced with the prospect of developing business from an under-developed network, what do you do? If you are not part of an organized network, I suggest you participate in some type of organization, association, religious institution, or other community group. Contact your college friends for ideas and connections. Get invited to an association for financial executives. Join a charity and serve on the board. Start your own group. Do SOMETHING. A successful benchmark for your first year of networking would be to develop a solid A Core of three to five people. Often emanating from this core will be additional, substantive contacts.

Referral Risk vs. Reward

What are the primary reasons that professionals hesitate to or actually resist making referrals? Some of the main issues include:

1. Professional's perceived risk of a bad outcome exceeds the anticipated rewards.

2. Referrer does not feel confident about making any referral.

3. Professional does not have enough trust in the known resource(s) to make a confident referral.

4. Client is difficult, especially with professionals.

5. Referrer seeks direct and immediate reciprocity, which may not be possible or practical.

6. Professional wants to receive but not give.

7. Professional is afraid to make a mistake.

8. Resource's personality may not mesh with the prospect.

9. Referrer's profession (e.g. legal and banking) adheres to a fiduciary standard that can easily dissuade making many referrals.

10. Professional has a fear of losing a client or close contact.

The following is the ultimate question many people ask: What form of guarantee is there that the referrer will exceed my fears (perceived risk) and perform well? Obviously, there are no absolute guarantees. One of the best ways to answer that question is to ensure that you know and trust that person enough, sometimes by vetting him or her with someone who has worked with him or her.

As a trusted advisor and COI, my sources know that I will never embarrass them and only enhance their relationship. This assurance makes me a low risk, high reward advisor. Second, I will make the referrer look good by reinforcing to the other party the solid character and expertise of my referrer. Lastly, I keep my referrer continually updated on the engagement progress, so he maintains a close relationship with the client.

"Referring professionals as resources to my clients is not the problem", says Marc Hankin, an extremely well-connected, intellectual property lawyer. "The problem is who to refer, since I know many of each flavor or type of professional." So Marc and I have the same referral issue common to the COI or well-known connectors. We agreed that we are excited when we are asked to give referrals and not hesitant to suggest someone who we know well to another party. The difficulty is determining the one, two, or three best resources out of a sea of potentials. Thus, Marc and I have established a similar approach:

1. Defining the prospect's needs to narrow the viable candidates – by geography (e.g. Los Angeles versus Ventura County), experience, personality, hourly rate or fee

constraints, complexity of the matter, ability to work on a team of trusted advisors, etc.

2. Best likelihood of successful results for the prospect.

3. Long-term relationship(s) with referred persons, both current and expected future.

4. Contacts on our "owed list" (i.e. who recently helped or referred us).

5. Most responsive to prospect's time constraints, if applicable.

Hankin's Number

Marc and I discussed the three cores, and his Hankin numbers. He believes his A Core is 25 to 50 people. He had not thought about a number for his B and C circles. His personal definition was that if you say their name aloud and can picture what they do or remember something about them, then that person is probably a "B teamer." By that definition, he estimated 50 to 150 persons in that category. His C circle contains 2,000 to 3000 people.

Marc also reflected that the A, B, and C categories probably are too loosely defined. What one really needs to determine is who from whatever "community" intersects. Thus, the real A's are those that one knows from a variety of communities. They fall into the overlap of communities, much like a collage of Venn diagrams. These could include:

*   referral partners
*   resources
*   friends
*   colleagues

- extended family
- great connectors
- clients

- one-offs
  - children's sports
  - alumni clubs
  - business clubs
  - religious institutions
  - weaker links – on your contact management system and reasonably well-known to you

My discussion with Marc made both of us reflect on our networking processes. It also reinforced the fact that, unless you have carefully analyzed your closest connections, you may forget someone when you most need to remember him or her.

Pareto Principle

Networking Pareto Principle

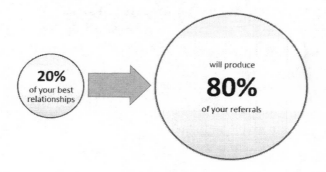

20% of your best relationships → will produce 80% of your referrals

In 1906, Italian economist Vilfredo Pareto observed that 80 percent of the land in Italy was owned by 20 percent of the people. He also developed the concept by estimating that 20 percent of the pea pods in his garden contained 80 percent of the peas. The Pareto Principle, also known as the 80/20 rule, states that roughly 80 percent of the effects come from 20 percent of the causes.

Many business people also use 80/20 as a rule of thumb, such as 80 percent of a firm's sales result from 20 percent of the clients. There is also mathematical evidence that many natural phenomena empirically exhibit an 80/20 distribution.

So what does this mean to you and your relationship-building program? It is likely that 20 percent of your best relationships will produce 80 percent of your referrals. But how do you know? One way is to ensure that your A Core is productive. And, you need to continually assess the B Core for additions to the A group. Your networking plan should allow for and generate face-to-face meetings more often.

The Pareto Principle can also be applied to a simple focus on the 20 percent of what is important, such as carefully allocating 20 percent of your networking efforts as follows:

1. Attend those functions and mixers with those you consider peers.

2. Reach out to key referral sources and resources.

3. Craft your blogs, website, and marketing materials to focus on your most profitable niche markets and services.

4. Make presentations to targeted professional service firms, learning how to insinuate them into your client base.

5. Continually analyze when and where "net work" is a better use of your time than "real work."

6. Become more well-connected to key people, and you will be more well-connected across a few communities. Building relationships is not a linear process.

7. Remain proactive by emphasizing the 20 percent of your services that provide the most profits.

Highlights

1. Determine the magic numbers for your A and B Cores. Keep the list fresh by analyzing it at least every 30 days.

2. Organize a comprehensive approach to tracking relationships to optimize your connectivity time.

3. Even senior corporate executives who are not owners are susceptible to "extinction" without a safety network.

4. Ensure that your A and B Cores know what you expect of them, and vice versa.

Chapter 5

FINDING YOUR MOJO

---

*"The world is full of magical things patiently waiting for our
wits to grow sharper."*
—Bertrand Russell

Finding your mojo really begins with a process of critical self-assessment — who you are and what you want. From that basic understanding, you can develop a realistic plan that effectively uses focused networking/relationship building to achieve your goals.

In developing your plan, analyze the keys to your successful networking. They will vary depending upon your immediate audience. Sincerity is one of the most important keys. Also, learn to naturally adopt giving as your most notable platform, even ahead of your professional skills and services. By giving often, as an everyday occurrence, you are producing your own form of karma.

---

*Anything even a little short of genuine
is very short of the mark.*

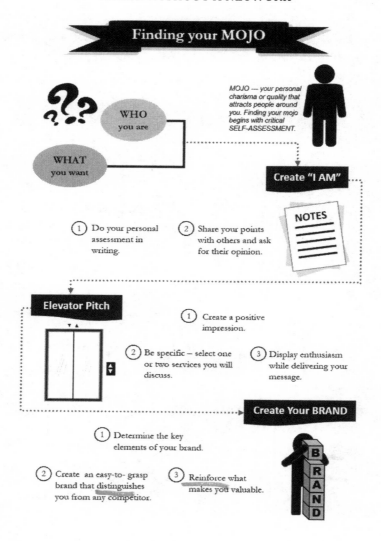

Who Are You?

My friend and deep thinker, Shel Brucker, told me the story of his introduction to Vistage. In order to become a group chair, he was invited to the San Diego corporate offices. Shel eagerly anticipated this new venture, after many years of serving as a corporate CEO. He was asked to introduce himself in a very different way. The question was: "Who are you?" He was surprised by the initial request and didn't know how to answer it.

"What stunned me was that this was the most fundamental question I had ever heard and I had no immediate answer for it," Shel said." Few of us ever get asked that question."

Upon first meeting someone, usually we ask, "What do you do? For whom?" How often do we really ask, "Who are you?" It's probably never asked because it does not seem appropriate. The question is so personal and requires the other person some time to think about it. Yet, how do you start to identify your values and to brand yourself if you don't know who you are?

Answering "Who are you?" is an exercise that will force you to do some honest thinking about yourself. It will also allow you to be inspiring in branding and introducing yourself. And, most importantly, it can provide you the confidence to make a professional connection with those you meet.

Creating "I AM"

Shel and I decided to create our own bullet point answers and share the results. I found the exercise very soul-searching and reflective. I am not suggesting that first or even second meetings should move in the direction of "Who are you?" I am suggesting that committing your personal assessment to writing is a worthwhile exercise. Show it to your family and friends who may challenge your points. Obviously, we are viewed differently by others than by ourselves. However, the "I AM" is a good first step to really understanding yourself and being able to share part of yourself with others.

My "I AM" sheet can be found in the Appendix.

Elevator Pitch

Your response to the following question is a key element of being remembered: What do you do? The elevator pitch is often the first chance to create a lasting impression. Done well, you advance to an easy-to-recall place in the receiver's mind. Done poorly, you may recede into the "woodwork." It is unlikely you will be memorable or relevant to the listener(s).

The best elevator speech should be practiced and honed into no more than one minute. The goal is to let your audience know who you are and how they should think of you. You should not be "pitching" yourself; rather, you are showing that you take pride in your services by the positive delivery of your message. In other words, what you convey will make some in the audience want to get to know you on a deeper level. It draws them to you.

The targeted elevator speech is never intended to enumerate each one of your service components. There are other ways, over time, to mention them. One of the ways for displaying the full depth of your services is to place bullet points on the back of your business card. When you hand someone your card, turn it over so that you can refer him to one or two of the services listed.

Probably the best way to decide your messaging is to select the one or two services you most want to get referred. Lead and leave with that. When you begin, make the opening statement impactful. While it need not shock our senses, it should grab our attention. As Deborah Shames and David Booth say in *Own the Room*, be specific because generalities make our minds wander: "Use specifics, rather than generalities, and paint a picture. If we can visualize your words, we are engaged."

Once you have engaged the audience, describe how you solved a client problem. Display your enthusiasm for the benefits or results you delivered, perhaps against formidable odds. Tell us a short, meaningful story with a tagline or phrase we cannot forget. What you have done is created word association with you and your professionalism. Your tagline can be "clever," so long as it is not too corny that it negates the powerful impact you have just created.

Leave your name and company for last. First, the audience is wrapped up in your energy and story and will continue to actively listen and anticipate hearing your name. When you start with your name and firm, the audience relaxes, and their brain waves are not as attentive. Second, they want to know and remember you. This "end placement" imprints better for them and serves as your closing statement.

The elevator pitch only works in a tall building, unless you capture your essence in a few words or sentences.

I suggest you vary your elevator presentation, so it does not become monotonous and forgettable (tuned out). Refresh the story, especially the opening. Maintain a strong level of energy each time, and the audience will be focused on your current performance.

An elevator speech is not a soliloquy. If it is beyond one minute in length, several things can happen, none of which are positive:

1. The audience "dozes," so little or no message is heard.

2. You may be considered a blowhard, not a trusted advisor.

3. Referral sources will be hesitant to introduce you to their clients, since you may show badly in front of them.

4. You could be viewed as rude and insensitive to others, who get less time to participate in a meeting.

PRACTICE, PRACTICE, PRACTICE. When you deliver in a relaxed, easygoing manner, you are more likeable and approachable. Thus, we want to deepen our relationship with you.

Creating Your Brand

A brand develops over time. The continual messaging via social media can drastically shorten that time frame. Brand awareness is initially based upon a visual – a logo, an advertisement, a commercial, a slogan or catchy phrase, or even word of mouth and viral marketing. We hear, and thus we see, or visualize a brand. That is the phenomenon of picturing what we hear or read. Thus, the brand is the perception of a positive expectation in the fulfillment of a service or good. When the ultimate delivery of the service is consistent and completely positive, the brand is reinforced.

A brand is anchored like a three-legged stool:
consistency, quality, and emotional attachment.

The following story depicts a definite transformation of a "fungible" lawyer into an unforgettable one. At a recent lunch, a lawyer related his moment of truth. Let's call him George. Before joining ProVisors, he had a strong corporate and litigation practice. But George recognized in 2008, at the beginning of the recession, that he needed more contacts, referral sources, and resources for his clients. He then joined ProVisors and attended his own group meeting every month. He never took advantage of the opportunity to guest at other groups or join one or more of the many available affinity groups (e.g. real estate, non-profit, manufacturers, human resources, etc.). Also, he was uncertain about presenting his service offerings and distinguishing himself. At one troika, he was asked about the types of clients he served. His response was mostly food manufacturers, distributors, and ancillary firms. Another ProVisors colleague, a marketing guru, told him to call himself The Food Lawyer.

At first, George had trouble with that brand, as he thought it was too cutesy and limiting. However, he tested it with a few professionals, and everyone loved it. It was so clean and so simple to visualize and understand. Thus, he rebranded himself and his firm. To this day, if you mention The Food Lawyer to a ProVisors member, that person knows it is George Salmas.

Unfortunately, most professionals do not have a clear or concise brand. They struggle to distinguish themselves. However, creating an easy-to-grasp concept or brand recognition should be the goal of each person, even the corporate-type. When we understand and remember who you are and what you are, our receptors are open to hearing more of what you have to say. We are more open to building the trust required for a lasting relationship.

Like George Salmas, you need a strong, easy-to-grasp brand to ignite and foster your career. It is necessary to establishing you and your firm as different from the competition. For example, I might say to a prospect, "Our valuation practice is unique in that nearly all of our professionals are very senior in experience and expertise." That statement clearly distinguishes us and demarks our firm from any competitor, most of whom are pyramidal in structure, with many junior people at lower levels within a hierarchy. It focuses on *who* we are, but does not demean any other company.

Your cogent brand message should create an emotional connection between you and the prospect. It makes your conversation less about impressing the prospect, and more about how you can deliver the needed service. In addition, it changes your focus from selling your service to hearing the needs of the prospect. It lays the foundation for how prospects and clients should think of you. And, it allows you to know more about who the buying prospect is, and how to deal with him.

A well-known, accepted brand allows you to position yourself away from the competition. It is a warranty, building your promise of integrity and delivery. It also provides a clear pathway to the types of clients you seek. It defines and connects you to those key referral sources and prospects that are within your market niche. When we really know who we are, it is easier to tell others how our services fit their needs.

Changing, refocusing, or adding a new brand can be very difficult to accomplish. For example, until 1997, I was not officially in the investment banking business. My firm's services were business and intellectual property (IP) valuations and asset appraisals. Even though in prior firms I was involved in some of the largest merger and acquisition (M&A) deals in the world and performed investment banking-type functions, I was never considered an investment banker.

So when we entered investment banking (IB) in 1997, my brand was clearly established as valuations and appraisals. Even after we closed some financings and sales of companies throughout the years, it was hard to write the extent of our IB expertise on the "white board". Thus, I know how long it takes to rebrand or expand your brand.

During the many years of ProVisors' existence (including the basic no-name group formations in 1988), numerous clients have been served by more than one ProVisors member. I believe the record number involved with one client was 12 or 13, occurring in the late 1990s. While that example is the extreme, it is not uncommon for three to five players to work on the same client issue(s). If referrals are readily made and positive outcomes are achieved, an organization can build a brand that is trusted and understood.

More than a few members have changed firms, and even careers, because of the power of close relationships, which provided a connection, pathway, or other critical assistance. Hundreds of millions of dollars in fees have resulted from the countless internal referrals. To accomplish the end of receiving access to someone else's clients, you must establish and reinforce your brand. Members are very forthright in asking one another for (and receiving) critical input, as follows:

1. Is my brand understood, at least in general?

2. Do you understand my primary services and industry focus?

3. Do you know or have I clearly stated my unique selling proposition (USP)?

4. If you were me, how would you explain my USP?

5. What can I do to improve my message?

6. Do I present information in a manner that is positive and well-received, rather than being classified as salesy?

7. Are there other tools available to me to process more effectively within ProVisors?

8. Am I referable for your clients? Can we play in the same sandbox? Can my firm and I represent you as the referrer?

Some key elements in furthering the acceptance and reach of your brand are as follows:

1. Remain true to yourself: be authentic.

2. Build trust by showing respect for the other person's viewpoint.

3. Determine your approach/style by careful preparation and practice.

4. Don't overcommit. Always deliver more than you promise.

5. Do not accept every referral or a lesser deal. Know when to politely say no.

Tools for Networking/Branding

There are many effective tools that can and should be used to convey your brand. Once you have determined the key elements of your brand, determine how they blend with those of your firm. Are they one and the same, or is your practice area just one of a plethora of service components?

Prospects buy your perceived ability to deliver value, first and foremost.

While you are always representing your firm, the primary deliverable is YOU. It is your attention to detail, accountability, likeability, respect for others, responsiveness, and overall quality of character that sets you apart. That delivery is also based on the prospect's feeling that you are the best solution to solve his needs. When you have achieved this rapport and bonding, price is a secondary consideration. However, if price is the primary criteria, then you must choose whether to pursue the prospect or not. If he does not really value your capabilities or deliverables, there is probably no upside to the pursuit.

We previously talked about niching your business, at least by industry. You may also consider niches in terms of fees. Is there a minimum fee criterion below which you do not want the business? If so, that line should be clear to others so that they present the most qualified referrals. Other delineators could include:

1. Industries or segments of industries that you serve and those you do not want to serve.

2. Specialties within your service menu that are clearly your strengths (e.g. for valuations, it could be a fairness opinion or estate tax gifting).

3. Revenue size of the prospect (or other criteria such as number of employees, cash flow/ EBITDA, etc.).

As part of your niche, focus on attending related association meetings, tradeshows, and conferences. Reach out to other industry experts to form alliances, or just learn from each other. Even "competitive" allies exchange business, especially when conflicts arise or they do not overlap with you in certain services. Write articles about successful client results you have achieved. Place these in key media (e.g. newspapers) and in trade publications. Deliver presentations that showcase your capabilities, as well as serving on panels for similar purposes.

One of the best and most direct ways to display your brand is at network meetings. ProVisors holds a variety of meetings, including but not limited to:

1. Home groups (meet monthly) – you can attend your primary group, as well as guest up to three times per year at any other home group.

2. Affinity groups – for example, in each major region of Southern California (i.e. Orange County, San Diego, Los Angeles, and San Fernando Valley), there is a Lawyers Only

group; these groups discuss a variety of legal-related topics and provide continuing education.

3. Mixers – open to any member (plus guests).

4. Social functions – these include one or more groups together.

And the list goes on. Well-organized networks create environments that give members numerous opportunities to convene and converse. At a group meeting, for example, there is usually an opportunity to introduce yourself (elevator pitch) and partake in the discussion topic. At every stage of a group meeting, mixer, or social group, there are opportunities to further the understanding of your brand. Ultimately, the way you present yourself — your demeanor, attitude, and willingness to share with others — is a significant part of solidifying your brand.

The Matter "On Your Desk"

Some professionals and executives are convinced that the immediate client or company matter "on their desk" is the most relevant means to connecting with others. To them, making reasonable and timely decisions regarding priority projects and engagements is more important than cultivating a new contact. Their logic is as follows:

1. When you take action and resolve issues, you can readily earn respect from clients and co-workers.

2. The manner in which you collaborate with others (e.g. the client's other trusted advisors), can create and solidify meaningful relationships.

3. Sharing clients and how you interact and display your professionalism is one of the most enduring forms of authentic networking.

4. Developing strong business friendships with their trusted advisors is essential to executives who want to build a community. You need not be close to every advisor, but you never know when that "friendship" can be useful in your career.

The matter "on your desk" can be a key component in building your relationships. However, if you do not exploit the potential connections, then the matter just becomes an excuse to not leave your office. You must still take the initiative to see how you can help these cohorts during the project.

A friend and long-time referral partner, Bill Weintraub, related an excellent example of focusing on the client matter and the other advisors. Bill is an estate tax attorney with a substantial practice comprising very wealthy clientele. During the estate planning for one particular family, Bill managed the team of advisors that was responsible for creating a comprehensive multi-generational plan. Among the advisors was a very young wealth manager. Bill made time to involve him in the entire process, akin to serving as his mentor. Since that time several years ago, this now more experienced wealth advisor has referred numerous clients to Bill Weintraub. Bill remarked that his collaborative style of treating each advisor and participant with respect has obviously paid dividends.

Scheduling Appointments

I believe that many people are put off by the task of scheduling appointments. The first and most prominent impediment is that the act of reaching out to someone can be scary, especially if you have not been in close touch with that person. Our initial reaction is "what if he rejects me or does not want to meet?" You need to get past that basic fear of rejection or you will never take the scheduling initiative.

He who schedules the meeting makes himself vulnerable, but often receives the accolades.

The second most common reason for not reaching out to schedule is simply inertia or laziness. It is easier to stay in your office and do real work than make an effort to "net work." We so often take the easy road, just because it is easier and less stressful. Whether we are busy or not, our excuse is that we do not have the time to meet others, especially if there's no direct or outstanding need.

Another excuse for not setting up meetings with others is that we do not have a passion to connect; we are satisfied with our place in life and do not need another boring meeting. Besides, we convince ourselves that there is probably nothing we can get from making and attending another meeting.

Still others feel that the actual process in setting and resetting appointments can be a huge waste of time. As someone who spends a lot of time scheduling, I will confirm that it does consume a part of your day. Those who resist the "appointment dance" do so at their own peril. They are probably defensive about not reaching out, usually with this type of attitude: If someone needs me, they can contact me. As discussed earlier in this book, that isolation from building relationships can leave you vulnerable and unemployed.

The first step to getting out of your comfort zone is extending yourself. The more we push ourselves, the closer we are to personally growing and self-actualization. We create a positive energy that translates into bettering our brand and station in life. Nearly everyone you reach out to will thank you for initiating the connection. These axioms apply to everyone, whether a service provider, corporate executive, or college student.

The process of active scheduling is not linear. It is vibrant and constantly in flux. Even when you have scheduled a meeting, you or the other party may change the schedule when a more important need arises. The person who makes the change is not necessarily "bad." Stuff happens, and if our appointment is changed, we need to remain neutral and not worry about why we need to reschedule. Just do it.

The most important rationale for being the instigator in setting appointments is that the receiver is nearly always thankful that you took that initiative. You did something for that party that she may have wanted to do, but did not. In instances where the other party does not know you well, or at all, it is imperative that you carefully connect the dots. You need to provide the reason(s) that the other person should take a meeting and how she can benefit from it. You may also need to explain some connection that unites the two of you, such as attending the same college, having mutual friends or business associates, etc. The use of LinkedIn can also increase your odds of getting the appointment.

One Sheet

Another way to present your message is by creating a complete profile that can be forwarded to prospective referring sources and clients, as well as putting one on LinkedIn. I suggest, in addition to your comprehensive website, that you create what is called a one sheet. As opposed to a brochure, lengthy résumé, or several pages of information, this simplified document is literally only one sheet of paper (front and back, if necessary) that describes who you are and the benefits of your services, as well as a clear, direct rationale for why someone would want to meet or refer you.

Typically, the front side provides brief descriptions of each major service you provide. A picture and short bio are also included. The back or reverse page often contains examples of client successes, again in abbreviated form. Some professionals use client testimonials in place of the client stories.

The most important part of the one sheet is the opening sentence, which follows a clever headline. This opening should be short and convey why the reader wants to know you. It is not another benefits statement. Rather, it is an appeal to someone as to who you are, your essence, and how the reader can visualize introducing you to his or her client(s) as a worthy, trusted advisor.

In addition to a one sheet which identifies each of your primary services, use this format to introduce each major service. When someone wants to know how you participate in an M&A transaction, put your panoply of M&A activities on a separate one sheet. When a prospect wants more information on just M&A (as opposed to general counsel or litigation legal services), use that tailored one sheet. For the M&A attorney or investment bank, consider a one sheet that shows recent client deals, with a brief description of each. No one wants to wade through page after page of written paragraphs that describe you. Use bullet points and short descriptions whenever possible.

LinkedIn Profile

In *Startup,* Reid Hoffman reiterated the well-known adage that each person is only six degrees (contacts) of separation from connecting with anyone of his or her choice. He further states that LinkedIn has reduced that adage to three degrees. LinkedIn contains well over one hundred million of the world's professional population, which now exceeds one billion. Those stats translate to the three degrees metric.

One of the better features of LinkedIn is your profile. Keep it fresh and current. Other advisors and potential clients will refer to it as part of their background diligence. In some cases, your LinkedIn information is accessed as much as or more than your website.

Numerous connections are made on LinkedIn. In fact, currently it is the best business resource for contacting all types of people, both professionals and corporate officers. The system provides instant access to related connections and diligence via your profile. You can easily ask others on LinkedIn to verify someone's credentials, as well as to provide access to one or more of their connections.

Website

There are many iterations of websites. Carefully select the one that best depicts the professionalism of you and your firm. A poorly created website may be worse than none at all.

One issue is whether to list clients. Obviously, the answer partly depends on whether you may, need, or want to get releases from them. Some professional licenses restrict the listing of clients or client testimonials. If you are not restricted, you should determine if revealing them provides an open door to your competitors. If you get the client's approval, naming a recognizable company as a client greatly outweighs the small risk of exposure to predators. What are you really sharing that helps a competing entity? Probably little to nothing.

Other considerations for creating or modifying your site are as follows:

1. Video — 1-2 minutes of each key person sharing their story.

2. Flashy or Staid — probably neither, or somewhere in between. The background and home page should represent a professional and current image.

3. Clear Menu Bar — with easy access to each element of the site.

4. Blog — short, direct, and current, as well as a call to action.

5. Service Descriptions — keep them simple.

6. Client Results — notable service accomplishments.

7. Collaborations — best trusted advisor links, and why.

8. <u>Key Personnel Résumés</u>

9. Interaction — an important, interactive way to respond to inquiries.

10. Type and Size of Client — focus on your primary markets.

Troika Meetings

The term "troika," which was previously described, is a three-person meeting that facilitates and fosters deeper relationships. It is probably the best way professionals can get to know and trust one another. At these sessions, members learn about someone's personal life; critique each other's elevator pitch or branding techniques; determine how they can help; figure out the major service components of someone's practice, including any focus on industries or client size; suggest a connection to another professional; trade stories of adding value for their clients; and assess whether the person can and should be referred into their client base.

You do not need an organization, such as ProVisors, to arrange your own troikas. You can help two people with some direct linkage and invite them to a troika where you attend. Many times when I encounter someone at a restaurant or business function, they thank me for a prior introduction that I made years ago, and what it meant to them. Often, I have forgotten about that connection, since I am continually referring people to each other. Every human being must have a gene or brain chip that allows us to remember who connected us. For some reason, that act of giving is by far the most memorable.

After the troika, be responsive and proactive. If you said you were going to make a call or contact someone to make an introduction, do it. Maybe you want to send a note or pertinent piece of information after a meeting. One meeting is usually not enough. If you feel the relationship can or should develop into a referral or resource ally, meet again in a short time. Send updates about your practice; new cases you have worked on to show how you can be helpful to referral sources and their clients; remind each other about professionals who help build your practices; make new introductions; and share innovations in your field.

One-on-One

The troika was designed to allow for less direct communication, whereby each person shares part of the conversation. As one person is speaking to another, the third person is attuned to that discussion. If that person wants, he can then interject as a means of keeping the flow of ideas alive. It still allows each person to talk enough so that the others learn something about one's professional and personal life. For some people who are less sure of themselves, the troika allows that person to ease into a dialogue. He does not have to "carry" the discourse, but merely contribute occasionally. This third-wheel position is usually less threatening, and he can learn how to communicate with more senior participants.

When is the one-on-one most beneficial? Almost always, since these sessions are arranged by one (or both) of the parties to deepen the level of discourse. Assuming these parties can or want to do business with one another, much more is accomplished in a shorter period. These meetings should be arranged often with our A Core players, perhaps once per quarter. Meeting one-on-one is always best when more personal matters can be revealed, and/or when one person is seeking direct and immediate help with a vexing issue.

I have met some skilled professionals who are surprisingly more comfortable presenting to a large group than being in a one-on-one setting. I guess they can talk more easily to a large audience about their business and services than about themselves. The innate ability to conduct a comfortable exchange with another businessperson is key to your success. How else can you convey your personal brand in a meaningful way, as well as offer to give something to the other person? When you get out of yourself and focus on what you can offer, you are a well-appreciated giver.

Social Media

How will Millennials, so comfortable with digital connections, step out from behind the machines and communicate directly? And does it matter?

Social media is continually changing.
Find your comfort zone and use it.

What we do know about Millennials is that the top five drivers of engagement for the high performers are the following:

1. Information Transparency – requires access to data to perform better and make decisions about their careers.

2. Corporate Strategy Attachment – wants a direct line of sight to perform according to a firm's mission and to know their work has purpose.

3. Opportunity – clearly sees a path to professional development and career advancement.

4. Visibility – most engaged when they have direct contact with and learn from the experiences of senior executives.

5. Personal Recognition – expects to participate in and receive rewards for programs that are personalized and recognize their time and efforts.

Today, a lot of business is conducted at such a rapid pace via the Internet. We cannot possibly meet face-to-face with every contact. But what was the genesis of how that business originated? I contend it is largely based on referrals from people known to the ultimate purchaser of the goods or services.

In our valuation and appraisal practice, I like to personally meet with every referrer/resource. The highly connected referral source with many clients is my ideal contact. Thus, a meeting reinforces the fact that, in selecting you, they chose wisely. Sometimes, because of timing or location, we get clients via email or telephone. And we get those clients because someone I know well and/or have done business with has highly recommended me and the firm. At times, that "strong referral" started with or was part of a "chain referral" (more than one person referring me) to someone else. However, someone in the linkage was willing to push for us, or at least add our name to a list of two or three. And, it is rare that we have not personally met someone in the chain.

Whenever possible, and even after we have completed a valuation assignment, I like to arrange a personal meeting with the client. First, a well-satisfied client is a number one fan and will pass our name along to business associates. Second, I like to determine why the client selected us and how he perceived our service. Third, I want to learn something personal about him or her that gives me insight as to how I can help. Fourth, that person's firm may need follow-up valuations or our investment banking services (capital raise or sale of the firm). Fifth, I want to find out who are his or her key trusted advisors (e.g. employment attorney, corporate attorney, CPA firm, etc.). Perhaps, he will contact them on my behalf, since one of them may not have been our referrer. At a minimum, I will contact and meet with these advisors. Sixth, as part of the conversation, he may think of other business executives and owners who can use our services.

The various forms of social media have made networking less of an art form and more of an organizational necessity. Do you have a plan to network: a strategy, an approach, and end goal(s) to connect with others?

I suggest you get comfortable with the forms of social media you know and like. For example, I am not on Facebook or Twitter. Perhaps that is a generational thing. I have chosen not to use these mediums for my connections. For millions, they work well. For me, they are a waste of precious time. And to what end do you stay in touch? Is your interfacing about you and what's going on in your life? *Building viable networks is more about creating value for others*. How does sending someone a selfie show up on the "giving scale of life?" We need to be very careful that outreach to others via social media is more about them and less about ourselves. When we get out of ourselves and are open to receiving what others offer, we can develop truer and deeper meaning to the relationship. It also clearly tells us if the other party is a substantial person with whom we really want to connect. Learning early about how and what we want to pursue (or not) in a new connection is so critical to focusing on positive, impactful activities and relationships. Eliminate the following from your world as early as possible:

- Takers – one-way willies
- Time wasters – cannot get to the point
- Phonies – enough said
- Surfacers – lacking depth or substance
- Socially awkward – too much work
- Disrespectful – respect is the key to a relationship
- Arrogant – the worst
- Untrustworthy – what else is there?
- Boring – know one of these?

The lasting relationship is premised on trust and chemistry.

Find a solid platform to select, refine, and maintain different types of relationships. Develop your own groupings, but do develop a systematic way to differentiate your key relationships. The following are possible delineations:

1. Referral Source – could send leads; introduce you to other service providers or people on your level (e.g., CEO to CEO).

2. Casual Contact – likeable, with some "chemistry" that easily reconnects you after some time lapse; may or may not be a source of business; probably a weaker tie.

3. Resource – person you want to refer to others, such as your client; good to excellent reputation for delivering what he promises; you probably do not care if the person reciprocates, especially if his business is not directly aligned with yours.

4. Database Outlier – you ping this person with periodic information, such as notices of completed engagements (aka tombstones); possibly after some time elapses or in the right circumstances, this party could move into a more prominent role for you, and vice versa.

5. Friend – may be a strong business connection, just someone to "face time," social contact, or more casual contact; within the "friend" bucket and those with whom you share the deepest chemistry. This could be the one you call at 3 AM in an emergency; obviously, for these people you do not even need a category.

6. Advocate/Fan – we all need advocates who tell others our good traits and only want the best for us.

7. Partner (Ally) – these could even be competitors who have somewhat different services and with whom you share referrals. Primarily, these are the A Core (Inner Circle) that you probably think of most often. You know each other well and will continue to dig deeper into that knowledge base, especially as you share clients. You refer each other the highest-level client with no hesitation. If practical, you should meet personally on a routine basis.

8. Client – could include relationships with several people employed by your client.

Meaningful relationships are based on shared personal feelings, experiences, and passions. We need to stand in the other person's shoes, and "see" and feel who and what they are. That perspective provides the empathy necessary to build a personal bonding. My friend Andy Wilson said, "As I strive to get more things done, I have become more aware of the power of networking." No one is an island. Your relationships are part of your professional balance sheet; they are springboards for getting things done.

In order to really deepen a relationship, we
need to give something of ourselves.

Andy is beta testing a software system called Rexter. While I won't do it justice, the conceptual framework is much more than just a contact management tool. Rexter fills the void between the LinkedIn connection and linear management process of classic CRM systems. With the web, our networks have exploded; we need new tools to help realize their potential – our memories and intuition simply cannot scale to keep up. Rexter captures your intuition about your contacts and, based upon the relationship group into which you place them and other criteria, the system automatically reminds you who to contact and why. Rexter becomes your "relationship GPS." How many of us remember whom we spoke to a couple days ago, not to mention to whom we should be proactively reaching out? Not many.

Regardless of the technology (and Rexter is ahead of the curve), we must organize and systematize our networking mode of operation (MO). And we must "go deep" with our partners, especially. From a business perspective, we should know the following about our key contacts:

- Primary competency, as well as secondary skills and services

- How best to collaborate, assessing the current matters, challenges, and results

- With whom their personality best matches (more on this in the *Showing Up* chapter)

- Markets served – size and industry focus of clients

- How strongly they are attached to you and refer to you exclusively or in a group (two or three) referral

- If they meet your client service standards, as well as keep you informed about what is ongoing with your client (your client is your capital)

Always carry business cards, even to family events or non-business gatherings. If you have a card and the other person does not, you will find out quickly if there was a real connection when you receive an email contact from him or her. When you receive a card, make notes on it, including the date and function. These notations could include a personal description, types of clients, which core group you place him or her in, personal action you promised to deliver, etc. When you are the one who should initiate the first follow-up, do so immediately, or in not more than one to two days so that your conversation is still fresh. Your responsiveness is a clear sign of accountability and your respect, as well as a nice way to accelerate the relationship development. Be relevant to the other person by your diligence to perform small, initial tasks.

Some describe the initial meeting as speed dating. Andy Wilson calls it HVN, for high velocity networking. The idea is to quickly determine the relevancy and potential value of a new contact; define a follow-up process; exchange cards and vital nuggets about respective interests; and move to the next contact. That does not mean you rush through the brief encounter. You mindfully engage and then move on when the potential isn't there or a solid connection is not made. The goal is to make connections at this stage, so don't attempt to close the deal on the first encounter. Maintain solid eye contact, not looking at their shoes or over their shoulders for the next person to meet. I call it authentic networking, meaning you move at a measured pace to make a few meaningful connections at any one encounter or meeting. Do not lose focus. The authentic networking exchange is based on Focus, Focus, and Focus.

Networking is personal and experiential. We learn a great deal by making the extra effort to talk or meet with our contacts. Remember this: in the age of the connected web, it is not just contacts that will make the difference, but those contacts we proactively develop into quality relationships. When you try new branding ideas or a revised elevator pitch, pay close attention to the other person's reaction and body language. Ask for honest input. Search for new ways to help, give, or share with others. As we matriculate in the networking process, be alert and stay flexible. Adapt to new circumstances. Adopt the attitude of a perpetual Beta, à la *The Startup of You*. Stay alert to new client opportunities, as well as job changes or starting your own business. Be an Alpha Dog that acts like a Beta.

So, what about the younger people who want everything in pictures on their devices? To many of them, networking is a selfie, tweet, or Instagram post. Will that be the future, where a face-to-face encounter is replaced by face on a device? No one knows, except that there is just no substitute for a personal touch and connection. Those who now spend many hours in front of the computer may someday need to learn viable inter-personal communication skills.

Highlights

1. Creating a clear, simple brand message is imperative to making you distinct and memorable.

2. A good brand creates a positive emotional connection with the receiver. Promulgate and test your brand with others, and even people who do not know you well.

3. Make use of all available tools to convey your brand. Focus on your uniqueness, such as responsiveness, service components, client size and industries, special expertise, and being a frequent giver.

4. Take the initiative to schedule face-to-face meetings, especially to listen and learn about the brands of others. These acts of outreach will be viewed positively.

Chapter 6

BUILD IT RIGHT

*The bravest are surely those who have the clearest vision
of what is before them, glory and danger alike, and yet
notwithstanding go out to meet it.*
—Thucydides

They Will Come

"**B**uild it and they will come." While this commonly known phrase may not always be true of a new business, it is when you are creating the BUSINESS OF YOU. Establishing a plan of attack is essential to building your brand identity. Your plan does not have to be too detailed; however, the act of planning is important in establishing your networking approach. How much time can you take away from your everyday work to connect with other people? Your plan must also allow for some down time (i.e. travel, email exchanges, etc.), including "wasted time," meetings or communication that's not always meaningful. However, we can still learn from those meetings that turn out to be unfulfilling or not fruitful. What might we learn? If nothing else, we definitely learn about ourselves, including one or more of the following:

1. Our approach with this particular person was wrong or misguided.

2. We were unfocused or uninteresting.

3. Our attitude was off, or we were not on our "A Game."

4. We need to practice our messaging.

5. Our elevator pitch is not succinct or easy to understand.

6. We are nervous, but we don't need to be. Almost everyone has the same feeling. The difference is how you use those nerves.

7. We were not an active listener.

On the other hand, none of the above learnings may apply to your unfulfilling meeting. Sometimes, you just need to accept the fact that there was not a strong connection, without rhyme or reason.

Direct Link

A "direct link" is a relationship with a referral source who shares a natural affinity to exchange business with you. A direct link is very valuable to you, much more so than a random connection. You need to carefully cultivate direct links as you develop business relationships, so that both parties can provide timely recommendations when needing to fulfill a prospect or client need.

One of my direct links is a long-standing friend and colleague, Doug Levinson. Doug is a well-educated and savvy strategic consultant. His firm is called Strategy That Rocks. A former investment banker, Doug knows precisely when to connect me with a prospective client. Over lunch one day, Doug and I were discussing his biggest professional challenge. He stated that his natural (and good) instincts, based upon his business experience, are both a blessing and a curse. They allow him to quickly understand a prospect's business and the key metrics for its successful growth. He consults with many early stage and tech firms, each one searching for the Holy Grail of information to create sustainable revenues (and profits). Doug's biggest problem is "seeing" the answer too quickly, often in the first 10 minutes of an introductory meeting. If he blurts out the answers, he often loses the strategic consulting assignment.

Upon hearing his dilemma, I had an epiphany. I told Doug a favorite anecdote of mine provided by a dear friend and mentor Gene Brown. Before he passed away, Gene was an accountant. When asked about his firm's fees, Gene always said his rate was $10,000 for the first hour. After that, Gene would say, his services were free because he only knew about an hour's worth of pertinent information.

After relating that story to Doug, I suggested he try a similar approach with a prospect at the first meeting. When the question of fees and how he charged was asked by the prospect, Doug would say the following: "I expect to provide solid advice or answers to you in the first hour, and that will cost $10,000. After that time, my advice is free."

We both laughed at this seemingly ridiculous approach to setting a fee for services. A few weeks after that humorous lunch, I saw Doug again at a networking mixer. He raced across the room to share an incredible story.

Doug said that at a recent introductory session with a tech startup, the company's president explained their metrics for driving revenue. As soon as Doug heard and analyzed that data, Doug realized that was the wrong approach. Rather than readily volunteer the correct metrics, Doug paused and offered an explanation of how he charged fees. Doug delivered the "$10,000 for the first hour" message, only to have the tech executive exhort a half-hearted laugh. They continued their dialogue, and Doug told him the best ways to monetize the business. Though slightly dumbfounded, the executive thought about Doug's response and agreed with him. Their meeting ended soon. One week later that executive sent Doug a check for $10,000!

BUILD IT RIGHT

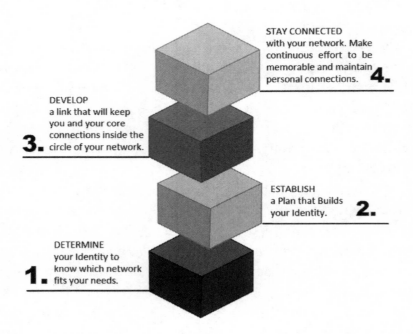

STAY CONNECTED with your network. Make continuous effort to be memorable and maintain personal connections. **4.**

DEVELOP a link that will keep you and your core connections inside the circle of your network. **3.**

ESTABLISH a Plan that Builds your Identity. **2.**

DETERMINE your Identity to know which network fits your needs. **1.**

Indirect Link

When you go to meetings with those not considered a "direct link," you can still provide value to these contacts. These meetings also add to your brand value. Your reputation grows from more people who know and support you. For instance, at your business or community network, you should contribute to the discussion, so you are viewed as open, thoughtful and approachable. One of the best ways to know who is going to attend the meeting is to get the list ahead of time. In addition, show up early and stand near the entry door. Essentially, you will become the group's early greeter. It will be hard for people to ignore you or, at the very least, not acknowledge you.

There is no specific timetable for when you like and trust someone enough to build a lasting relationship.

Another important aspect of connectivity is likeability. One factor that contributes to someone's likeability is simply being warm when you meet. Another means to being likeable is focusing your attention on listening to the other person and determining how you might be able to help him or her. This form of unsolicited generosity makes a lasting impression and increases your likeability.

At a first meeting, do not expect to develop a meaningful relationship. A certain amount of accountability is critical to connectivity. Ensure that you are deliberate in your style and always looking to help the other person. If you are consistent in that approach, over time others will consider you accountable. Another factor in being considered accountable is following through after you promise to do something for someone. Let's say that you meet someone for the first time at a meeting or a mixer. You then suggest to the other person a contact that you think they should meet. You agree to make that connection, probably by email. Being accountable means you immediately follow through after having made the promise to connect them.

For some people, successful networking is a learned process. For others, it is as easy as waking up in the morning and starting to communicate with people that you meet daily. No matter your style, your willingness and ability to smoothly network will improve over time. Interestingly, even some of the most senior executives have told me that they are sometimes awkward or self-conscious in a group setting. They said they are most comfortable with those whom they communicate or interact on a continual basis. The most rewarding stories come from those who overcome their initial aversion to group meetings, and now look forward to them.

One of the important rules of expanding your network is to address and conquer that which you fear.

How do you know when you are well-connected with another person? A good gauge is whether you feel comfortable asking him or her for help or assistance. It is obviously easier to ask if you are referable into their client base. It might even surprise you when they say that you are not, mainly because you do not have enough experience in a certain market or in your profession. But at least you have taken the bold step to find out. The worst case is when you really don't know how you stand with someone, but you continue to pursue a connection that may turn out to be a waste of time.

As professional service providers, we should know our best direct contacts or links among other professionals. We know the type and specialty within a particular profession that are appropriate as resources for our clients. We also know those who are relevant to us as referrers of business. Some people, in order to conserve time, focus solely on those direct links that are either referral sources or resources. I firmly believe that they could be cutting off other potentially valuable contacts. Many of us have examples of random meetings with professionals outside our direct links that have provided some of the most beneficial and profitable client referrals.

"Real Work" is not "Net Work"

What defines "real work?" Is real work the actual production of a good or service? Then, the "net work" necessary to create the "real work" opportunity is also real work. There is the age-old debate about the relative importance of sales versus engineering (or outside versus inside) personnel. Nothing happens without the client or customer. At the same time, there is no sustained customer without the delivery of timely and cost-effective service. Both types of employees are important.

Neither side of this debate will concede much ground; the important role of management is to acknowledge any apparent divide and provide solutions that bridge the gaps, so that the participants act for the common good of the business. My contention is that "net work" is as arduous as "real work," and often more frustrating. In networking, you will often meet and "kiss many frogs" before a real relationship develops. Then, when the referrer calls with a prospect, it is often perceived by the inside "real" workers that the "networker" did nothing. He may not be part of the billable client service, so his schmoosing appears to be fun, easy, and not "real work."

Networking is a process, one that should be integrated into your daily life.

Perhaps you are primarily an in-house employee doing "real work," and securing or sourcing clients is not your immediate responsibility. Typically, if you confine yourself to your work station, you may fall short of the most successful positions in the firm. You will only reach the higher tiers of success when you have developed a "book of business" or A Core of relationships.

I purposefully delineated "real work" from "net work," since the concepts apply to any business environment. You need not be a professional service provider to focus on or harness your networking skills. For example, a CEO requires access to people, information, and resources to:

1. Stay abreast of marketing, products, services, pricing, and other trends in the marketplace.

2. Learn about financial alternatives and sources.

3. Develop strategic plans.

4. Become and remain informed about competitors.

5. Recruit key executives, advisors, and professionals.

Begin the networking process by developing a list of key individuals in your company. What persons, information, or resources do they require access to in order to better perform their job responsibilities or fulfill the strategic objectives of the company? Identify the types of networks or organizations that might benefit each individual, as well as how and where to access these networking opportunities.

Numerous articles have been published about how people find a job. It is well-researched and known that more than 80 percent of senior job placements are directly related to a contact or connection with a person known to the recruiter. That makes complete sense. So one of the understated but critical aspects of networking is the building of a community that can help you personally. Such help can be manifested in any number of ways – from job seeking to life-saving doctors, and everything in between. Build your connections, friendships, and communities so that you always have resources for any need.

A vivid example of how strong connections may be vital occurred in one of the ProVisors groups. The discussion topic was to describe something personal in your life. One person mentioned that her daughter in another city was dying of a serious condition, one that had not been diagnosed. She further described the symptoms of the critical disease. We were all depressed by the news. Three people in the room that day provided incredible medical connections – two internists with specialties in the same category of disease that were located in the daughter's city, as well as a third high-level contact at the Center for Disease Control in Atlanta.

At the next monthly meeting of this same group, the parent happily reported that one of the medical connections provided after the last meeting had diagnosed the disease and was successfully treating her daughter. The group broke out in applause. Nothing is more fulfilling than finding a solution to a contact's personal problem.

I have talked to many corporate executives about their networks. From my experience, most have worked inside of corporations for the majority of their business careers. Some of them have joined industry associations or groups, while others belong to religious organizations or alumni clubs. All of these networks are important for individuals in Corporate America to stay connected and to secure future employment opportunities. The key is to stay involved. There is a tendency at the highest management levels, especially the CEO, to close himself off to outside contacts. I think some of this reluctance is a fear of outsiders "selling" to the CEO. However, if the CEO is not the majority owner, she is as vulnerable to being fired as any executive. It is important that the CEO and other corporate types stay well-networked.

One last story about "real work" versus "net work." Some time ago, I participated on a panel for a bar association (legal, not drinking). The topic was "Networking Tips for Lawyers." In the audience was a younger lawyer who had recently moved to L.A.

from New York. His question to the panel was how best to break into the L.A. market. In answering his question, I first asked him if he was single, since that would have a bearing on my response to him. He said he was. I then asked if he knew of the various network organizations in and around L.A. He did not, so I mentioned a few. But my real answer to his conundrum was for him to turn his regular day and nighttime hours upside down. I suggested that he do most of his legal work only at night and on weekends. His hours from early morning until early evening would be devoted to scheduling meetings and attending those one-on-one sessions. His adopted mantra was to "never be alone in the daylight" (similar to the book by Keith Ferrazzi entitled *Never Eat Alone*). I still do not know if he followed my advice, but the takeaway was for him to find a way to network and create referral sources. His circumstance was similar to mine in 1987.

Remember: There is no one path to successful networking. In fact, it is so individualistic that there are likely as many paths as there are people.

At the back of this book is a list of networking do's and don'ts. Networking is a lifestyle and relatively easy for those who truly understand and enjoy the time spent building relationships. However, even the most savvy, experienced professionals may be inept at the process.

Staying Connected

One of the true gurus of networking and a longtime associate of mine is David Ackert. While writing this book, he met with me to provide encouragement, critical input, and a fresh outlook. David is a business development and branding coach who provides excellent weekly tips in his blog. One of his writings spoke to the notion of Revenue Routines, which propagated consistency of activity. In other words, we should not make excuses for doing the "real work" versus the "net work." David suggests that business outreach must be so repetitive and ongoing that it is second nature, like brushing your teeth. David provided the following list as minimum monthly activities:

- Schedule lunch with a prospective client – 4/month
- Schedule lunch with a referral source – 2/month
- Write a blog post – 4/month
- Host a supper club – 1/month
- Produce a webinar – 1/month
- Spend 20 minutes on social media – 8/month
- Deliver a live presentation – 2/month
- Attend a networking event – 1/month

The key to maintaining your enthusiasm is a consistent focus on the things you hope to achieve.

In addition to the above ideas, David encourages each person to define in writing how he will sustain enthusiasm for networking. When we commit to a goal, our subconscious mind filters out the stimulus that is not related to our goal, which in turn motivates our performance in pursuing the goal. Neuroscience tells us that this performance-enhancing sense of focus, renewal, and drive comes from our motivation to pursue something specific. Here are a few techniques that will keep your eye on the ball, even as day-to-day distractions compete for your attention:

1. Set up visual reminders of your goal. Place a relevant photo on your desk or a sticky note on your monitor so that your goal stays top-of-mind.

2. Schedule monthly goal-review sessions. Put this in your calendar so you have a regular check-in with yourself to assess your progress.

3. Enroll an accountability partner. Work with a professional marketer at your firm, an outside coach, or a colleague who shares your ambition and engages you in a regular discussion about the advancement of your goal.

4. Share your goal with a mentor. Choose someone you respect, so that whenever they ask about your goal, you are motivated to report progress, lest you disappoint them.

Ackert's outlook is similar to mine, in that our networking outreach activities are done as part of our lifestyle. Business development is not a spigot to be turned on periodically. Rather, it is a continuum of habitual acts that, the more we practice, the easier and more naturally they are accomplished. As a result, you become a highly regarded and sought after person. You become the professional Alpha Dog, willing to give and receive with aplomb. You create your relevance no matter what age — young or old.

One of the items or activities on David's list is a monthly dinner club. I have talked to several professionals and executives who participate in dinner clubs. Some of the clubs are ostensibly about the food or wine, but others are also about connections or community. When you meet regularly with a group of peers, the natural flow of camaraderie and kinship can lead to deep friendships or even business.

Additional Communities

Another form of community is business groups such as Vistage (formerly TEC). Business owners and executives meet in groups without competitors, and serve much like each other's advisory council or board of directors. The businesses are far ranging in type, but mostly small and middle market in size, say less than $100 million in revenue. These groups average 10 to 15 members, facilitated by a leader, who meets regularly with each participant in between the monthly meetings. The members get current and unfiltered advice related to the issues and problems they present to the group. Some direct business flows as a result.

Another previously identified group is the Young Presidents Organization (YPO). This elite group has more than 21,000 chief executives in about 125 countries. Members are highly screened to meet certain criteria, such as company revenue size and whether the individual serves as a CEO. The purpose of the monthly meetings is for education and idea exchange, but obviously many key friendships are forged and business sharing results. The international aspect appeals to many YPO members, as they travel to foreign destinations to mix, mingle, and receive high caliber, educational presentations. Many functions outside the monthly meetings are arranged for family members as well.

Smaller, ad hoc groups for professionals are arranged to brainstorm how best to collaborate among the members. The principal commonality or theme of these mastermind groups is helping each other (paying it forward) and creating karma. When appropriate, business referrals and relationships ensue.

Staying meaningfully connected does require work. Sometimes we have to push ourselves out of bed or the office to participate in these communities. Often the result of "doing" is rewarded, even if the benefit is not immediate or recognizable at the time.

One contrarian viewpoint is that a person can network too much. I have heard the comment, "she spreads herself 'too thin' and may appear to lack substance." Glad-handers are like "fish in the barrel." They may begin to look fungible (homogeneous) and too easy to ignore individually. Wherever or whenever you show up, show up well. If everyone at the mixer is too familiar, it may be time to change your pattern of attendance or the functions you attend. Getting scarcer does not mean dropping out; it may mean revamping your branding message and emphasizing another aspect of your service or personality. Beta test a "new you" and remain flexible as your networking evolves.

Here are a few additional ways to staying connected:

1. Start a blog, but make sure you contribute on a regular basis so your readership can follow you.

2. Join a LinkedIn group. Stay associated with persons in a related field (affinity), learning new ideas to apply with your prospects and clients.

3. Join a charity, and serve on the board.

4. Teach part time at a college or university. This activity will sharpen your professional communication skills and rejuvenate any lost "fire" or passion to network. It also gives you a certain level of credibility.

5. Coach your children in their sport(s).

6. Start a network group – dinner or lunch club, mastermind, referral based, etc. When you do, you must be willing to spend the requisite time to select and persuade the right people to join; vary the meeting content; stimulate the expression of those in attendance; revisit the benefits to members and revise or adapt as necessary; allow others to take ownership and organize the sessions; share the cost

or even make a profit; never stray too far from the original group intent or mission; and, attract top-level players who attract other talent.

7. Participate in family-centric events and activities.

8. Write a book (or two or three . . .), like me.

Whatever you undertake, stay alert to how your community involvement is impacting you. Are you personally growing? As a result of the interpersonal actions, are you learning how to better express yourself? Ask others for feedback as to how they perceive your message and messaging. Your group activity should enhance your personal progress – increased self-confidence, better listening skills, improved understanding of business, etc.

Second, be aware of the centers of influence (COI) or opinion leaders around you. Are you close to them? Can you help them in some way? By way of example, one of the first things I hear from a newly appointed group leader in ProVisors is how others view them. While the group leader did not really change his or her approach, suddenly the group leader's importance to others was elevated. Those who accept leader status are rewarded in many ways. Group leaders or drivers in any organization should receive and enjoy the fruits of their leadership, such as one or more of the following:

1. Stature. As a center of influence (COI), her counsel is sought by other members. The group leader must likewise rise to the occasion, not letting her new power override her prior modus operandi. The group leader is there to serve her membership and to provide guidance to members as to how to become more impactful net givers.

2. Vortex of Referral Vetting. Professionals now ask the group leader for his or her opinions about other members' credentials, style, etc.

3. Enhanced Member Contacts. Members will naturally ask the leader for her perception on a variety of matters. Included in the panoply are ideas to help the member accelerate her progress in the network.

4. Group Leader Input. The group leaders should meet together at regular sessions. At these meetings, a myriad of ideas may surface. Thus, the leaders can continually share best practices and assess how much the participants are gaining from the group sessions.

Top of Mind

Even though you now have and follow a networking plan, it is only a roadmap. It ensures that you carry out the activities that are acceptable to you. Hopefully, your plan requires you to push yourself by scheduling maximum daily or weekly contacts. The "real work" will get done around and in between the network. Your thoughts impact, control, and become your actions. Thus, think "net work," and "real work" will follow.

Your primary goal is to be continually top of mind to others. Short of implanting a memory chip within another, at least be known as the frequent giver.

What else makes us relevant and memorable — and top of mind? First, be yourself. Second, be present and aware of reaching out to help others. Help comes in small and large doses. Part of it is being sensitive to each individual with whom you are in contact. Third, demonstrate a caring attitude and leave a positive impression in your wake. At the same time, do not indulge the insincere, boorish time-wasters.

A vivid example occurred many years ago at a ProVisors mixer, which was open to all members. A lawyer, who was naturally shy, was in attendance. I give him credit for attending his first event that included about 200 people. When I saw him (and I already knew him), I instinctively walked across the room to talk to him. I decided he could benefit from being introduced to certain professionals. I guided him over to a small group, introduced him to each of them, and walked away. The next time I saw him, he was smiling and talking easily with a new group of professionals. Today, he is an outspoken proponent of how positively networking has affected his business and personal growth.

High-trust relationships are critical in today's environment.

Another way to be memorable is to establish and repeat a catchy phrase. The trick is to not be too corny. Maybe you have a story or anecdote about a client success that you created. Keep it short, pithy, and visual. We need to "see it" to remember it. For instance, for our valuation and investment banking practices, we are trademarking, "We Deliver Value." It is an opening phrase that gets others' attention.

Do you know how others will remember and refer you, or your "Referability Quotient (RQ)?" It consists of your visibility, credibility, and suitability. Do you clearly define your primary services (one to three, at most) as they relate to specific clients and markets? You are not referable if others do not know the deal size and market(s) that define you. Focus on clarifying your message and showing others that you are a low-risk, high-reward referral.

What is your RQ if you work in Corporate America? How is an executive referable, and what does that mean? One way is to be visible to and known by other employees and managers. The most successful company cultures have incorporated various forms of interconnecting their personnel. One example is bringing different departments together to dialogue and move toward understanding each other. Too often, people confuse the functions of marketing and sales, using the terms interchangeably. Some firms bring these groups together to share strategy. Each department should support the other, such as marketing needing feedback from sales personnel, who learn about the effectiveness of the marketing campaigns directly from the customer or client.

Recently, I spoke at length to a tax accountant and partner in his CPA firm. He mentioned that his career path was atypical. He received an MBA and Master's degree in tax, and started in industry as a controller. He held chief financial officer positions in three companies, which spanned the first 16 years of his work-life. Then, he left corporate life to become a partner at his current accounting firm. We discussed his tenures inside the three companies and his unwillingness to connect outside his firms. He never went to events or networking functions. Looking in his rear-view mirror, he now realizes that he was vulnerable. As Ron said, "I was too busy to be smart" about networking. His head was "down" as he worked at his job, and he never worried about his position or inherent susceptibility to becoming unemployed. He was without a lifeline of solid contacts to open other doors. Today, Ron is determined to not repeat his past lack of outreach or inactivity. He is now a well-known professional based upon a focused networking approach.

In the book *Give and Take*, author Adam Grant suggests he has discovered the most connected person in the world, Adam Rifkin. Adam is a venture capitalist in Silicon Valley (where else?) who is the master of the "two-minute favor." He provides honest feedback and introductions to help others. His mantra is to develop a network that creates value for everyone, not just himself. Rifkin is continually available to strangers of substance, helping them with connections that directly lead to employment or other opportunities. He serves without seeking reciprocity. He makes no effort to keep score or to determine if his referred connection is optimal. He is like the Duracell Bunny for connecting, perpetually moving people along to their next destination.

Grant describes an interesting anecdote involving Rifkin. When Rifkin needed help with a particular project, he chose not to involve his friends, family, or inner core of colleagues. He really wanted critical feedback for the project and felt those closest to him would water down their criticism and only support him. He decided to expand his outreach to his looser ties, people he had much less interaction with on a regular basis. These people were those not intimately part of his business or personal sphere. The amazing revelation was that some of the looser ties were positive that he contacted them. He got the help he needed for his project, and more.

It also provides an important lesson to each of us. Weaker ties still need periodic nurturing. Many times, someone is a less direct tie only because the relationship is newer and not so focused. I have seen many of these people catapult into my inner circle, literally overnight. Many times this occurrence was based on a well-timed, mutually beneficial success.

How do you become an expert networker? In *Outliers*, Malcolm Gladwell posited that expertise is developed when you have practiced it for more than 10,000 hours. Broken down, if we practice our techniques for two hours per day for 250 work days each year, we will have mastered the proper skill set in about 20 years. So get started now. In reality, we never master networking, since we can learn nuances and subtleties every day that expand our ability to communicate and connect.

One of the best tactics to stay "top of mind," or at least "re-enter the mind" from one's memory bank, is to be interesting. And, the best way to be interesting is to be interested.

People flock to unique, interesting, and inspiring people.

Being interesting is exemplified by showing genuine interest in the needs and wants of others. We cannot always offer a solution or sage advice, but we probably know someone who can. Do not be a door stopper; be a door opener. Seek out contacts that close gaps for others. At the same time, maintain the confidentiality of others when you receive personal information from them.

As you progress in your networking, others will be drawn to your giving persona. Within your comfort zone, determine if a referral has a much larger payoff than the risk involved in making it (meaning that the referred professional does a poor job). If so, make it willingly.

When you are given a referral to a new prospect who becomes a client, that client is the referrer's capital. Always return to the original source for new resources needed by that common client. Or at least establish the flow of information back to the referrer based upon what he asks from you to keep him informed. At some point, that client may become more yours than the initial referring source. However, you must get an agreement from the original referring source that this client is equally shared or considered more yours. At that time, the client can rightly be termed your capital. The baton is then passed.

Highlights

1. Self-assessment is the first and most vital step to start a short- and long-term relationship creation plan.

2. Your level of confidence will increase with every personal encounter. The more positive your attitude, the better you will deliver your message and engage the other person(s).

3. "Net work" is part of "real work." If we have no customers or clients, we cannot perform "real work."

4. Your time is under your control, as long as you meet the goals set forth for you by your firm. Start your business development efforts early in your career, and you will *never be alone* in your professional life.

- Chapter 7 -

PROACTIVE CONNECTING

The greatest danger for most of us lies not in setting our aim too high and falling short, but in setting our aim too low, and achieving our mark.
—Michelangelo

What do I mean by proactive connecting? Simply put, it connotes getting out of yourself and reaching out to build allied relationships. When you know who you are and your brand, you are naturally more open to conversing with other professionals or executives.

Proactive connecting, as part of authentic networking, should be viewed as a long-term approach to developing more business, especially the kind that you really want. Your plan should include both referral sources and potential clients.

Part of being proactive is merely taking action to enable better situations and potential outcomes for you, rather than waiting for something to happen. One manifestation of being proactive is to produce content marketing. Rather than just a "ping" to check in with a contact (client, prospect, or referral source), provide something useful. The suggested range of information could include:

1. Industry trends and new market niches

2. Data on competitors in their industry

3. Legislative developments

4. Executive movement/notable comments

5. Relevant industry transactions

6. Recent client success stories

In addition to merely highlighting or linking the contact to the above information, place this information into a blog. Your commentary suggests you possess a certain level of expertise, which also allows you to subtly relate the issue back to your services.

As David Ackert suggests, content marketing or outreach is a form of "auditioning for the part" and displaying to the receiving party what he can expect when you are hired. The method is also part of your branding, which can create an emotional bond with the reader. The more the reader consumes your information, the more he elevates your stature. At some point, he not only accepts you and your brand, but also imagines you as a trusted advisor.

Demonstrating Value

Do you have a goal to demonstrate value every day? While that is probably not possible, such a goal can set a positive tone for your career. Do you want to merely "get through" your work day or do you want to continue to earn the respect of those you encounter — employees, bosses, co-workers, clients, prospects, and referral sources — by your work ethic?

Your attitude about delivering quality and value to everyone should not be understated. Even after we are hired, we are still auditioning for the next gig. I think of networking or building connections as a continual dress rehearsal. While we have memorized our part, we can always improve our delivery. Also, we can always elevate the performance of our fellow actors by enhancing their lives.

Meeting in Person

If talking with someone is important enough to you and the location is favorable, you will find a way to meet in person. You can also accomplish a significant amount of sharing via phone or email. The word of caution to email correspondence is that it is discoverable, as well as subject to misinterpretation or possibly even upsetting to one party. In contrast to phone and email conversations, ideas and information flow more naturally in a face-to-face meeting. Often, the best of these encounters results in an emotional bonding that almost never takes place in a digital forum. Usually, new ideas emanate from the back and forth exchange, and often the most novel and creative solutions are based on this type of collaboration.

Part of positive proactivity is remaining even-keeled. The outreach is not about your needs, but those of the other party. It is not a time for closing the sale; rather, the outreach ensures that you stay relevant and memorable. Then, when the timing is right, the prospect almost cannot help but think of you. You have branded yourself as the go-to person who provides value.

The Right Time

Some people truly believe that they do not have to develop a network. They may have ascended within the family business, regardless of their outside connections. Or they may have so few clients that "net work" is more of a burden than a blessing. My supposition is that one should always remain open to making quality connections, since you never know how you may be impacted.

By way of example, consider the story of a friend and trusted advisor, Marla Merhab-Robinson. During college, she worked for a company where the majority shareholder was a friend and client of her uncle, who was a lawyer. While Marla attended law school, that firm merged with a public company. Fresh from passing the bar, Marla joined the public company as executive vice president and in-house legal counsel. In this corporate environment, she did not need to market herself for work. She became an expert in transaction and securities law.

About three years later, her company was sold. Marla matriculated at a law firm originally started by her mother and two uncles, one of whom was the aforementioned lawyer. She continued to practice corporate law, serving as general counsel to many firms. In addition, she added employment law to her practice, which was a natural fit with her in-house counsel work. During this period, Marla developed relationships with select trusted advisors, who she referred to her clients. Since she had a cadre of resources, she did not join any networking groups.

Six years later, Marla started her own law firm, and her former client base followed her. For years, Linda Duffy, a good friend and member of ProVisors, tried to convince her to join the organization. Since she had a solid cadre of resources, Marla resisted. When Linda became part of a new group that was forming, Marla was finally convinced to help build that group.

At her first meeting of the new group, Marla met an attorney, Ken August, with a practice similar to hers. However, he also had a specialty she did not possess — international law. Since that early connection, she and Ken have collaborated often for mutual clients. Subsequently, Marla reached out to the ProVisors membership and hired an estate tax partner, Paula Clarkson. From no prior formal networking to her immersion into ProVisors, Marla is now an outspoken proponent of continually being open to building many key referral and resource relationships with high-quality professionals and people.

Collaboration

In our company, the best example of collaboration among service providers is during the sale of a business. Most sales involve a long-term process, often six to twelve months from the signing of an agreement with our investment bank. Part of the reason for that length of time is that there are many parties and advisors on each side of the deal. Also, lenders and investors now perform more tedious due diligence than in the pre-recession days before 2008. This diligence can require the expertise of numerous trusted advisors.

The investment banker (IB), accountant, and M&A lawyer are, though not all-inclusive, the most obvious advisors to a seller. To achieve the best price and deal terms, these parties need to be in sync at all times. The more complicated the seller's operations, the more critical the use of and collaboration among trusted professional advisors. This section provides an example of how advisors can and should collaborate, and when that seller "train" needs to switch to a new track (e.g. change an advisor).

Client

The client, call them Plasticman, was a manufacturer of plastic containers for consumer use. Their products were sold via a small internal salesforce, as well as a wide distribution network. The customer base included 30 medium to large firms, with a concentration of 70 percent of sales in five customers. Revenues for the prior fiscal year were $60 million, with an EBITDA (earnings before interest, taxes, depreciation, and amortization) just over $8 million. Capital expenditures were sizeable each year, mostly to modernize and replace equipment. The products were made in Los Angeles and Lincoln, Nebraska. In Lincoln, Plasticman was beset by attempts to unionize.

Securing the Client

Our investment bank (IB), Mentor Securities, was referred to Plasticman by three of their advisors – the corporate attorney, outside accountant, and business banker. These three sources knew me and our services well. To secure the client, we competed with two other firms. Our primary edge was being strongly referred by their three closest advisors. I had developed these relationships both within and outside ProVisors. Also, I had previously referred the banker to two other prospects.

Before meeting with Plasticman, I spoke to each referral source for personal insights about the company's management. The banker knew the owners the best, so he was able to share "intel" on the company's structure and personalities. Plasticman had been a client of the bank for twelve years. The corporate attorney had attained this client two years prior, primarily to review contracts and customer agreements. At that time, he had also referred in an intellectual property (IP) lawyer to ensure that the patents and trademarks were protected throughout the U.S. and select countries in Europe.

In my conversation with the corporate counsel, he mentioned that he had little to no M&A transaction experience. We discussed possible referrals to the client to handle the sale transaction. He also informed me of the relationship of the primary owner, the father (CEO), and his son, who was chief operating officer. The son owned 30 percent of the common stock.

The third advisor was the tax accountant. He knew that the son really wanted to buyout his father, setting up a potential conflict in the sale process. At the same time, the accountant also mentioned that the father and son had a strong bond and worked well together. The son reluctantly approved the sale process, hoping to remain with the buying group in a prominent position. I also learned from the CPA that his firm provided only compiled financials.

My son was designated the lead professional. Thus, our father-son team was a nice match for Plasticman's similar ownership structure. We agreed upon a minimum price for the sale, with an expectation of an upside from the right buyer. We also agreed that, once hired, we would analyze what other advisors they might need to prepare the company for sale. We explained that our extensive resource base was a pool from which professionals could be selected by them.

Seller Due Diligence

Preparing a seller for his one big event — the sale of his company — must be handled carefully and cooperatively with the client. There are a myriad of potential resources to refer into this process. For Plasticman, we determined with the client that they first needed an M&A transaction attorney. We suggested two attorneys that were proficient, matched well with their personalities, and were nearby their main office.

The next professional service provider to consider utilizing was an accounting firm that would perform an audit. While we expected that the selected buyer would want their own audit, we wanted to present a scrubbed seller. Prior to the selection of an auditor, we suggested the client hire a financial consultant to analyze their records and cleanse them. They chose one we recommended. The client then interviewed three accounting firms, two of which we referred. Once the senior financial advisor had prepared the financials for audit, the client hired an auditor.

The client had no ERISA issues per se. However, confronted with labor union advances in Nebraska, Plasticman sought and hired an employment law firm well-versed in union organizing. In addition to warding off the union, the employment counsel reviewed HR (human resources) procedures and compliance, especially in California. In turn, this counsel requested the hiring

NAKED WITHOUT A NETWORK

of an HR consultant to perform the more tedious diligence on personnel matters and files. We were instrumental in arranging the interviews for both the counsel and HR consultants.

Another advisor we brought into the process was an insurance risk expert, primarily to analyze the potential product and other liabilities. This risk assessment was needed to allow the seller to make certain representations and warranties in the purchase agreement. We also wanted to know the costs and coverage necessary to support the seller's exposure.

We conducted our own diligence of the company, as a basis for writing the Confidential Information Memorandum or Book. At the same time, the tax advisors discussed with the owners how they could minimize taxes. One approach was to contribute some of the shares to a charitable remainder trust (CRT). To qualify for a charitable deduction, the contribution must be made prior to executing a letter of intent. To expand the range of creative tax minimization, we recommended the services of a federal and estate tax attorney and a wealth manager. The client decided to retain his longtime wealth manager. Of the two tax attorneys we suggested, the owners selected one.

The above sale transaction provides numerous examples of how professional service providers can and should be referred into client matters. Without the power and presence of an organization such as ProVisors, we would not have so easily fulfilled our important role as trusted advisor.

Board of Advisors

Nearly everyone should consider an informal or formal board of advisors. The simplest form is probably a group of friends who meet on occasion. What if even that setting was expanded to include a focus on helping one another? Would that change the group mix or viability? If you are part of a friendship circle that convenes for parties, dinners, sports events, etc., you may not want to disrupt the group's natural flow. At the same time, you should assess if some of these friends are suitable for a more focused "business" group. However, splitting off some of the friends for a separate reason may cause irreparable damage to the group as a whole. Longtime friendships are not easily replaceable.

In organizing your board, think carefully about who will fit well and why. Then, determine the mission(s) of your board. The best kind of board is one where each of the members feels that the board is really about each of them.

Your original Board might include persons with whom you do *not* do business. Why is that a consideration? In some cases, business associates many not want to expose their own vulnerabilities or be privy to yours. While I do not think "closeness breeds contempt," you must carefully vet your candidates for that possibility. What if a close business relationship felt slighted by others on your board? Worse, what if you rejected his or her best, most heartfelt opinions or advice?

All of this discussion leads to first determining if you even want a board of advisors. I have never organized a formal or informal board. Yet, I have a close circle of confidants, including my wife, who I consult with often. Usually, my issues are presented to people who are particularly trusted in an area of expertise or experience, or both. I assume that my thoughts or opinions are subject to questioning. When I seek advice, it is not just for confirmation. It is to be challenged and to enhance my thought process.

If you decide to convene a board, start first with a clear mission or vision of why the group is meeting. Use the first meeting to fully explore the range of advisement you are seeking. The easiest type of board to organize is one that addresses your business — strategy, operations, services, personnel, etc. You and the members may also decide to serve as each other's trusted advisors. Broach the subject of how much the orientation of the group is business versus personal, as the two often intertwine. Obviously, our personal attitudes and experiences will play out in various business settings. The most energetic and fulfilling board will readily tackle all matters — personal, business, or both.

Once your mission is clearly understood, the most vital part of the meeting is the sharing of information and opinions. We usually learn the most about ourselves from the honest feedback of others. Each participant should want to be challenged and even exhorted to improve his or her state of mind and output. This form of sharing reaps ultimate benefits, since it is given and received with the best of intentions.

Another suggestion is to create an agenda prior to each meeting. That way, there is a theme and focus. You might rotate the leadership and hosting of each meeting. Each member should have a portion of one meeting to present his or her challenges and receive unrestricted feedback. Also, each member should be willing to be heard on the deepest level he chooses.

Mentoring

One way to improve your visibility and center of influence (COI) status is to serve as a mentor to others. That is one of the highest forms of giving, with no expectation of reciprocity. At the same time, when you help someone's personal and/or business growth, you have created "goodwill" and "guilt." These "g" words are like reservoirs and may well be released by the mentee as payback at any time.

Mentoring can occur in numerous ways and settings. One such approach is to provide guidance to someone in your firm. In addition to enhancing his or her professional or job skills, show him or her how to better engage and communicate with people at all levels in the hierarchy, and outside the firm.

As an executive, the best way to work yourself out of a job is to mentor the top recruits and performers. The more depth in the management ranks, the stronger the firm. Creating executive time to plan and provide company vision is often a luxury. When practical, make it a reality. The top-performing executives and owners have found ways to leverage their roles, allowing themselves time to think and plan. That way, you will not only work in your business, but can work on your business.

Mentoring and seeing someone else succeed is not just thoughtful; it is immensely satisfying. It is much like the movie *Pay it Forward*, in that you as the mentor (payor) feel fulfilled. Those of us who help others accept and practice personal responsibility give a lasting gift, and each of the parties impacted by this mentoring has improved.

My most vivid and personal example of a mentoring relationship resulted in a positive outcome for both the mentor and me. Let's start with the mentor. I met Gene Brown, managing partner of his mid-sized accounting firm, shortly after starting The Mentor Group in 1987. Gene and I met often to discuss business and personal issues, as well as sharing advice on managing our firms and business development strategies. Gene even had a few of his partners join PNG in the 1990s.

Based upon my close relationship with Gene and his partners, our firm served as their prominent (nearly exclusive) valuation go-to firm. We also helped train one of his partners to perform business valuations, since the accounting firm wanted to expand their service offerings for smaller clients.

Gene spent a lot of time grooming his younger partners to succeed the four older name partners. He was preparing the firm for their retirements. At some point, Gene suggested that a merger with a larger firm was their best exit. Soon thereafter, I introduced him to the senior managing partner of a much larger firm. Although in our investment bank we receive fees for connecting buyers and sellers, I did not even consider taking a fee because of my unique relationship with Gene. The moral of the story is that the mentor helped the mentee, who in turn helped the mentor.

You never know just how impactful your mentoring may be, or who really reaps the most benefits from this type of relationship.

The Referral Dilemma

Since every firm is different as to how they "control" referrals, the safest policy is to know everyone. But is that practical? "Why can't I just concentrate my efforts on "my person" in that firm? He will always put forth my name for referrals of that firm's clients."

This is a real dilemma or conundrum. Recently, I met with a co-managing partner of a 20-person accounting firm. I know two of his partners well, having done business with each of them on several occasions over many years. Yet, I briefly encountered the "new guy." When we met, I mentioned a few of our services. He said that he knew and had recommended our competitors. In fact, he was a more active referrer than both of my other contacts combined. This scenario is not uncommon, which is why you need to continually expand your connections.

Unless your A Core is super small, you will often face a referral dilemma. There is no way any of us can refer all of the people we know well. Our goal is to keep refining our resources according to the following:

1. Friendship connection

2. Primary expertise

3. Personality style

4. Ranked/prominence

5. Age and experience

6. Industry niche focus (client type)

7. Size of client

8. Geographical reach

9. Secondary services

10. Most current referral(s) received

In addition to sorting and ranking your potential resources (those to whom you can give business), how do you resolve the broader issue of reaching as many potential referral sources as possible? Here are some suggestions:

1. Learn the internal process/politics of each firm you encounter. Is there a master list on which you need to be included? If so, are you included on a list which corresponds to each of your main service components? Who maintains the list and should you meet or entertain him or her?

2. Assuming there is no list, does the firm have unpublicized criteria for selecting resources? You should know how referrals are made at a given company. In firms of 10 to 50 professionals, the partners usually control the leads. You should ensure that at least the primary partners know you well. One way to accomplish this connectivity is to arrange a presentation with these partners (and others) to discuss how your services and theirs dovetail. Find out how best and when to insinuate them into your prospects, clients, and significant referral sources.

3. The other information you need to ascertain about the firm is how the partners are compensated for originations

of new clients. In some firms, individuals receive credit or compensation for business originations and/or development. If such a program exists, you may want to ask your key contacts if you should refer prospects directly to them, and not to other professionals in their firm. This conversation is most important and relevant to solidifying your A Core relations.

In large firms of more than 100 professionals, get to know the COI's (at a minimum) who directly interface with you. For example, if you are an investment banker, build a relationship with the corporate/transactional attorneys at that firm. In the long-term, there is no shortage of valuable connections you could solidify in the same firm. Obviously, you probably cannot reciprocate with more than a few. Again, ask these key contacts the best way to refer them work. At the same time, there are some professionals who do not care so much about direct reciprocity. If they are senior and highly sought for deals, they may refer you if they perceive that you are the best candidate for their client.

Highlights

1. Listen carefully to trusted advisors and how they serve their clients. Then figure out how and when you fit in so you can collaborate with them.

2. Analyze how you could use a board of advisors, and serve on one for someone else. This activity will often solidify both the personal and business connection.

3. Define your key criteria for referring a resource to a prospect or client. Refine these points as you get to know the resource better.

Chapter 8

SHOWING UP

It is necessary for us to learn from others' mistakes. You will not live long enough to make them all yourself.
—Hyman George Rickover

Being Memorable

To be truly memorable, it is not enough to be thought of as an expert in a particular subject or field. People must also remember you for your distinctive, positive manner. What we all grapple with is how to appear and reappear in a referrer's memory. There is no checklist to being charismatic. It is a quest that never ends. Rather than getting too frustrated with the process, continue to craft your brand message. Even while honing this message, you convey some form of your brand to the listener. That is why I suggest asking others to critique and refine your words and delivery so it makes sense to them. Remember, when we are in a state of focused listening — which is supported by clear communication — we are most open and alert to new ideas and people.

The following are some specific ways of becoming more memorable:

1. Always leave the best impression.

2. Send out an informational blog or email blast, or simply a reminder note every so often, at least to your A and B Cores.

3. Show up often so people see and remember you. Attend events whenever you can, updating your contacts and jogging their memory about your services.

4. Arrange in-person meetings. Check-in emails are a good way to set up these meetings.

5. Complete your LinkedIn profile, and update it regularly. Within the profile, highlight your uniqueness, using key words and accomplishments.

6. Serve on a panel or seek out opportunities to present to larger groups. At those presentations, provide a memorable story about one ideal client.

7. Continue reaching out to clients, friends, or co-workers to find ways you can help them.

8. Be a guest participator at network meetings.

9. Ask others to critique your current elevator speech, or a new idea you may have.

10. Develop your reputation as a "connector" by focusing a portion of each day on making introductions – both in person and via email.

11. Know your market size and type of client. It helps in your elevator speech and affirming your brand message. Support this information with numbers, such as "we serve companies with at least $10 million in annual revenue."

12. Reinforce two or three specialties and industries whenever you communicate your services to another person.

13. Survey your referral sources and clients to see what they may need. Send them timely information, and more than just a "hello" ping which often offers little value.

14. Every so often, search around on LinkedIn to identify trends or pending needs for potential prospects and prior clients.

15. Send a handwritten follow-up or thank you letter by regular mail.

Accepting Each Other

You don't need to be the expert at what you do. However, you should know and play to your strengths. The most important skill to display at any networking opportunity is what I call "active listening." Active listing means practicing the intention to be involved in what another person is saying, usually by asking clarifying questions. Unless you truly understand the other person's needs and point of view, it is highly unlikely you can forge a meaningful business friendship.

Many of us have completed personality surveys; most notable is probably the Myers-Briggs Personality Test. Does anyone remember the key components of your personality type? Did you ever discuss these at a professional workshop or with colleagues? These kinds of workshops are a fun way to learn about others. Also, they can provide useful information about communicating better with each other. While no one fits neatly into one personality category at every moment of every day, these assessments help us understand someone's general predilections.

In addition, one person can *act* in any or all of the various "personality types" depending upon (1) the actions of the other party; (2) emotional intelligence gleaned from that party; (3) attachment to good or bad news happening in one's personal life; or, (4) passion for the immediate topic, meeting, outcome, etc. In other words, the immediacy of one's surroundings may override his or her normal disposition.

One problem with type-casting other people (via formal personality assessments or by snap judgment) is that we may misread, underestimate, or limit our perceptions of others. For example, if John is a known or acknowledged visionary, we expect him to think and process in an idealistic manner. As described in *Own The Room,* visionaries usually have magnetic personalities and are often perceived to be great leaders. Martin Luther King Jr., Gandhi, and Moses are examples of visionaries who articulated compelling visions of the future. Their messages came from their core beliefs and commitment to those beliefs. Although visionaries can vividly describe the big picture, do not expect them to deliver the details. Knowing this about visionaries, should we always treat and react to such a person in the same way? Of course not. Perhaps one visionary has a practical side that also allows him or her to champion a direct course of action. She organizes her thoughts in a way that outlines the expected outcome and prods others to believe in the idea, concept, program, or plan, so that those responsible to implement the program are persuaded and encouraged to succeed. She may or may not create the process strategy to achieve the results, but she will coach the other participants to achieve the milestones along the path to success.

Most organizations function best when people have defined their core strengths and personalities. Assigning specific tasks to people of certain dispositions is an efficient method to completing any program or mission. But why do we need to put a box around someone's prevalent attributes? The simple answer is so we can better comprehend them.

When we type-cast someone, it is much easier to "wrap" our mind around his or her basic traits and expectations. We are then more comfortable assuming that the person will behave within a prescribed pattern. Thus, we know what to expect from him or her, within reason, which allows us to focus our energies on the issues at hand or what is immediately on *our* minds.

We all "profile" others, whether consciously or not. We have to; if we don't, our brains would be constantly overstimulated, and our immediate behavior will become potentially erratic. We will have a difficult time just relating to others without making any baseline judgment. However, while predetermining one's personality preferences is helpful for initially framing the interaction, narrow-casting someone many detract from your chances of building a deeper relationship:

1. Depending on the issue and their particular feelings and motivations, our approach to them may be too rigid. Worse, it may be completely off base.

2. If you are too focused on the stereotype with which you are dealing, and you think you should react in a certain way, you might come across as insincere.

3. Even with a basic framework of the personality type, let your intuition and natural instincts dictate your conversation. Listen and react to the other's cues. Do not communicate as if you have pre-determined how they will talk and respond. It is better to "get outside" yourself and your agenda. Thus, you will be more real and open to places in the conversation where your points, stories, or passions will be more clearly received. Remember, a person is most open-minded and receptive to you when he asks a question, not when you are in a tell mode.

Personality Types

Substantial research has been conducted to measure how people perceive the world and make decisions. The earliest of these studies, also known as typological theories, were completed by Carl Jung in 1921. Jung categorized all experiences according to the following: sensation, intuition, feeling and thinking. And, one of these four functions is primarily dominant or a preference, at least most of the time.

MBTI

Forty years after Jung's first study, Katherine Cook Briggs and her daughter, Isabel Briggs Myers, applied the theory of psychological types into practical use. To this day, the Myers-Briggs Type Indicator (MBTI®) is one of the world's most famous statistically validated communication assessments. The test determines how one's behavior is strongly influenced or even dictated by the way he perceives information and/or reaches conclusions. A four-letter score is provided to the test-taker:

- The first letter can be either E or I, which determines one's aptitude for socialization ("E" represents extrovert and "I" introvert).

- The second letter can be either N or S, which determines one's method of perception. "N" represents intuition or one who sees the bigger picture; "S" represents sensation, or how one perceives information in a more detailed sense.

    o Fact-gathering preferences often fall into either S or N categories:

S Preferences	N Preferences
Presents info step by step	Wants the big picture
Attends to what is said or done	Reads between the lines
Wants concrete examples	Likes abstraction & symbols
Wants practical information	Focuses on concepts
Wants brief responses	Like to see patterns
Goes to the bottom line	Likes variety and challenge
Gets right to the point	Dislikes detail
Likes action	Can be easily distracted

• The third letter can either be F or T, which determines one's thought pattern. "F" represents feeling, or how one is concerned with his effect on other people, while "T" represents thinking, or how one reaches conclusions via rational logic (thinking).

    o The two ways people reach conclusions are either T or F.

T Preferences	F Preferences
Present info logically	Comments are taken personally
Wants consistency & validity	Likes to talk to people
Prefers principles & law	Trusts and accepts people
Can be analytical & critical	Responds to human values
Clarifies by questioning	Tends to be warm and friendly
Tends to be business like	Might overreact to feelings
Tends to be blunt	Has difficulty saying no
Likes the formal approach	Needs to be treated personally

• The fourth letter can either be J or P, which determines one's preference when relating to the outside world. "J" represents judgment and "P" represents perception.

Generally, by understanding another's preferences, we are better able to predict actual behavior. The end result is that we can communicate more effectively, since we can anticipate how he will respond to our style.

Overall, there are 16 distinctive personality types in the MBTI (described in more detail in Appendix A). The types do not measure aptitude; they simply indicate an individual's inclination versus another. Of the four cognitive functions, one is generally dominant; then, there are the secondary (auxiliary), tertiary, and shadow functions.

The goal in knowing about personality types
is to appreciate differences in people.

The MBTI only measures one's preferences, not traits or skills. A clearer understanding of our unique preferences allows us to be more accepting of others' differences and, thus, relate better. As we apply this knowledge in our professional lives, hopefully we can develop and demonstrate the patience to deal with others who do not share similar personality preferences.

For the progressive networker, it is important to understand how your personality preferences interact with others. When you encounter opposites or incompatible or clashing personalities, you can and should adjust to accommodate the other party. That is not to say you bend your natural M.O.; it is to suggest that you adapt to and match other styles as a way of bonding. At the same time, don't let anybody force you to change who you are or how you present yourself.

My colleague and friend John Ambrecht, a tax attorney in Santa Barbara, has studied the impact of MBTI and its nuances on family dynamics. He is able to quickly assess the various personality types assembled within a family structure. He is certain that his ability to explain how and why each member reacts to another is a key ingredient to creating a successful estate plan. For example, in a family whereby one or two members are perceived as "difficult," the better explanation to an outsider may simply be that there are preference differences. Just the clarity to reveal that preferences are not difficulties usually releases the family interaction stress. It also works well as part of the grieving process after the death of a patriarch, when power shifts and family and business relationships automatically change.

Ambrecht delineates two categories — Rules and Roles — to better understand these power shifts within a family. He has then applied this theorem to his professional practice. Rules are those underpinnings of a social system which regulate human behaviors and interactions: they maintain some stability and fairness in society. Examples include business competition, traffic vehicles, estate and gift tax laws, government regulations, etc. They do not discriminate, but apply equally to everyone and everything.

Roles, on the other hand, are based on a ranking system (e.g. father-child, teacher-student, etc.) The higher you climb the proverbial ladder of success, the fewer the number of people. A Role in this context is the acceptance of your ascension to a specific position on this ladder that juxtaposes you in relation to someone else. Because you reached a certain location on this ladder, a Role also encompasses a set of actions you undertook to get there.

As it applies to Ambrecht's practice, it is essential that a family's dynamic and governing structure properly accounts for the "new family" Roles and Rules. Because of this, John counsels the participants to act as a business team. He suggests industry team-building and assessment tools to a family, such as the MBTI. This self-awareness from each family participant about others' preferences is a first step toward better collective decision-making by the family. The next step of changing the dynamic is usually self-acceptance, followed by openness and honesty. Each person must be willing to share his or her innermost thoughts. While no estate plan functions ideally, at least John and his team mitigate the actual and potential internecine battles. Thus, the success rate for his family plans is greatly improved.

MBTI Preferences

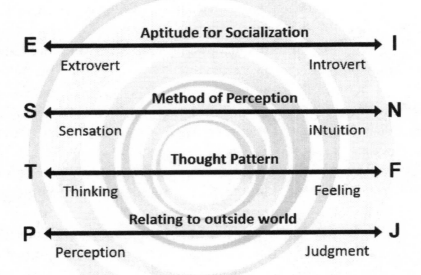

DISC®

The modern-day version of the MBTI test is known as DISC®. It is a much easier-to-grasp assessment of someone's personality style. Once you understand your "type," it becomes easier to recognize another's style. The four primary styles of DISC® are as follows:

- Dominance
- Inducement

- Submission
- Compliance

The originator of these four emotions and behaviors was psychologist William Moulton Marston in 1928. Marston postulated that each style is based on two perceptions:

1. Whether a person views his environment as favorable or unfavorable.

2. Whether a person pictures himself as in control or lacking control of his environment.

The following chart explains the four primary styles of DISC®. The bottom line in understanding DISC® is that each person manifests preferences and attitudes predominantly within his quadrant. Thus, each person's actions are fairly predictable, and you can improve your interaction knowing another's mindset and predispositions.

Some companies use this assessment to screen potential employees. Another good use of DISC® is the self-awareness it can bring to you and your interactions with others. For example, if you are referring another person to a client or colleague, what are your expectations of this person's approach and ensuing success with his new relationship? Another good application is for management of an organization: as CEO, whom can you identify for a specific team, project, or future leadership position?

In workplace and network environments, DISC® assessments are useful. Below are a few thoughts when using them:

1. If your profile (the way you answered the assessment questions) does not match how you see yourself, perhaps you need to reconsider your self-view.

2. The assessment is simply about one's priorities and preferences. There is no judgment about one's predilections; it is just how decisions tend to be made given general types.

3. One's priorities and preferences are greatly influenced by life experiences, education, and maturity. You are not beholden to any one category.

4. Each style is equally valuable, and we should learn how to better interact with each of the other styles or quadrants. For instance, it is interesting to note that the diagonal quadrants will most likely co-exist well, i.e. D and S, and I and C quadrants.

5. Sometimes, when you do not relate well to another person, it could be that one of you is stuck in a position or not understanding the other's style.

6. DISC® can also be helpful for internal team-building, as it clearly identifies ways to communicate so that the participants actively respect and listen to one another.

7. You can use the style differences in DISC® to cope with difficult people. The power of knowing who you are will help you remain centered and in control.

8. Think of the styles and quadrants in a depersonalized way, or as an objective observer. When you remove or lessen your emotional reaction to another, you can more clearly see the interpersonal solution(s).

9. As a leader, model the behavior that enhances your style. Do not allow a particular style to dictate your poor behavior.

10. Lastly, create an environment or culture within your organization that allows each person to maximize their potential in contributing to the overall mission and common good.

Different Strokes

While writing this book, I discussed the main concepts with a colleague. He brought up an interesting point. What if the person is better off remaining in the background or back office? If he is a competent worker yet shy or insecure, why does he need to be exposed to personal, face-to-face networking? Furthermore, what if this same person has some social anxiety and is fearful of new people and new situations?

There is no easy answer for the person with a physical or mental handicap that prevents their inclination to socialize. Still, I believe that nearly everyone can benefit from personal interactions. There are excellent coaches and communication trainers, as well as consultants, who are specifically adept at working with disorders.

DISC

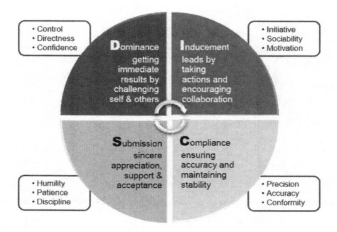

This latter group of people might merely accept the person as different, not as someone with a disability. Perhaps their path to improved social skills is a smaller group in which the participants feel safer.

In regards to the reclusive back office employee, what might be a solution to make him or her more inclined to face-to-face networking? Some form of training in communication skills is likely warranted. In *Own The Room,* the authors discuss how to involve these more reserved, but technically competent, people in marketing pitches. The more they are visible to a prospect or client, the stronger and more capable your organization appears. And, given an opportunity to perform, they may shine beyond even their expectations. Worst case, help the uncomfortable to get more comfortable by your outreach or assist them to form a peer group.

Referable

What can you do to stand out from others or become the most referable? These are key questions for a professional service provider, since that can lead to direct sources of revenue. Likewise, the corporate executive succeeds when she creates an aura of leadership.

Being referable is like winning a sports contest. The best prepared and most confident usually wins.

Part of the answer is how you "show up" or present yourself. Here are a few ideas for developing more meaningful relationships:

1. **Be Punctual**. If you are habitually late, you create the wrong impression. People do not view you as responsible.

They lose respect for you because you are implying by your tardiness that you disrespect their time.

2. **Dress Appropriately**. Comply with the generally accepted dress code for the interview, meeting, presentation, or mixer event. There is no reason to flaunt conventional modes of attire just to "stand out" or make a statement that you are different.

3. **Stay in the Moment**. Each of our lives is replete with numerous and continual ebbs and flows, both professionally and personally. Be diligent in maintaining your focus on the person(s) and task at hand. The most memorable people to me are those I have encountered who treated me as the only important person in their lives at that *moment*. Put away or turn off your phone and other devices when conversing with others.

4. **Hold to the Time Allotted**. Another key way to demonstrate respect is to remain vigilant about an agreed upon time for a meeting. Meetings often exceed the allotted time. However, you need to be the one upholding your commitment to a time limit. Do not get so caught up in your own goals and thoughts that you end up boring the participants and making them antsy to leave. And, most importantly, when you have reached an accord in your discussions, stop talking. Move on.

5. **Maintain Focus**. Learn how best to enunciate your points and opinions without wandering too far from the focus of your comments. For example, in networking meetings (similar to most gatherings), there are specific times to provide your "elevator speech." This is the time to *briefly* explain who you are and your business, not a time for a soliloquy. Like it or not, people will judge you as likeable or

referable based on the length of your elevator speech.

Brevity (conciseness) and noteworthiness are the most important components of your pitch. Did you share a short story about a client that really made you worth remembering? Did you share a moniker or catchy slogan to help others identify you?

Part of your elevator pitch can be used when you first meet someone. But instead of applying your 30- to 60-second pitch that may be appropriate in a group setting, reduce it to 5 to 15 seconds. Create a snippet that makes the other person react or ask a question. If this person does not respond, your "intro" may be boring. Practice these short and long "openings" so they flow naturally and without effort. Ask your confidants for their opinions on both kinds of pitches.

6. **Keep Up With Your Client**. If you do not have continuous, ongoing clients, you may only encounter them irregularly. Once a prospect becomes a client, the "hunt" is over. Thus, a client is often easy to ignore, as we are exhilarated more by the juicy new prospect. So, how do we reverse our natural inclination to pay less attention to existing clients?

If you are a public accountant or outside general legal counsel, for instance, your clients are usually under some type of evergreen agreement with you. Thus, you likely have a more routine or ongoing dialogue with them. Even these existing relationships may be tenuous if you are not systematic in making regular contact. Your outreach can be anything; perhaps suggest an operational or financial improvement. Or, introduce them to a vendor, potential customer, or referral source. Very satisfied clients are often the most regular source of new business and the best source to champion your services to others.

The concept of organizing a regular, periodic contact is

not only applicable to the professional service provider. For example, as a CEO or COO of a manufacturing or distribution company, what better way is there to retain customers or secure new ones than to meet with your largest and best customers? Organize special programs to acknowledge and reward them. For every retained customer, the cost of the next sale is probably 20 percent of what it might cost to land an entirely new prospect.

7. **Specialize**. While your firm may perform a litany of services, we will only remember one or two of your specialties. Our natural inclination is to not limit our service scope or offerings, nor identify only a few industries we serve. However, our *general* message often gets lost because of the overwhelming supply of data sources, websites, blogs, etc. No one can remember who we are or what we do, thus reducing our memorability quotient.

   Even if we provide 10 products or services, it is better to be remembered for two or three primary ones than not at all. It takes a real mind shift to make this transition to specializing, and then advertising it. When you deliver your elevator speech or introduce yourself, focus on one to three services or product components and the same number of industry niches. Tell creative anecdotes related to these areas of specialization, so the listener can mentally "grab" a handle or visual connection and retain it. What is truly retained will be recalled by our short-term memory.

8. **Earn Respect**. This is the ultimate place where everyone wants to land, since this is the most effective way to be remembered. But how do you earn others' respect? You start by showing proper respect to others. Another way to achieve respect is to volunteer for leadership roles within a group. Assuming a position of some authority will both

elevate your brand and allow you to know the members faster and better. It also empowers you to learn about and affect the group culture.

Respect is earned. If you respect yourself and manifest that persona, you will be treated that way.

---

9. **LISTEN, LISTEN, LISTEN**. Listen intently to hear pertinent information and cues to which you can respond. If your head is filled with an agenda to tell your story, you will probably miss communication cues from the other party.

The sooner you can find commonalities, the sooner you break down the walls or barriers we put in place to protect us. Do you think that your initial insecurity in meeting a new person is only happening inside you? No matter how outwardly confident a person appears, there is always a nagging fear of the uncertainty as to how another person will be received. The fear of interacting with strangers is probably second on our list of social anxieties, behind public speaking.

Once you have determined some common ground (e.g. similar interests or attitudes), a more meaningful dialogue can occur. As part of establishing relationships, agree to follow up and coordinate a meeting. Make a note on the person's business card about a key fact or tidbit you learned about him or her, and recall it at the agreed upon follow-up.

When you're in a room full of people and receive at least a few business cards, how do you remember the faces and names at a later point? Train your short-term memory receptors to zoom in on anything distinctive about an individual. Remember a particular type of client or industry mentioned. Use a technique to associate the person's name and face with a word or phrase that rhymes. Some people think I resemble former NBA star Jerry West. Since there is some resemblance, I guess it is one way people remember me.

It is far better to be a great listener than an incessant talker.

Remain at a function or event for the entire time. Most people will be quick to leave. Often, the stragglers will loosen up even more toward the end. This can be a good time to capture meaningful information. The beginnings of relationships often flourish at these times. And, once basic introductions have been made, the talk can quickly turn to real business opportunities.

10. **Give, Give, Give**. Your real agenda at a function or even a lunch is to learn enough about the other person in a short time period, so that you can offer to help him or her. Giving can take on many forms, such as:

   • Sharing key information that helps them solve a personal or business problem.

   • Offering to make a meaningful connection to another person that is of direct and immediate benefit. Once you have developed an expanded network of contacts, you can focus on sharing those contacts with others. When you agree to share, make sure you are timely in the introduction or connection. We all react positively to responsive and accountable people.

   • Introducing the person to a personal friend where they can develop a relationship. Do not be afraid to share your best resources with people you like and trust. Many times, people tell me that I made a key strategic business or personal connection for them. They seem to always remember, whether I made the referral in person or via email. I am convinced that our brain has a "chip for connections" that gets imbedded in our long-term memory. Your generosity is a form of karma, especially when you are giving without any expectation of an immediate payback. Be a net giver who does not need to keep score.

11. **Start Your Own Group**. Today, many executives and professionals belong to more than one community. These may range from country clubs to eating clubs, and religious institutions to charities. Each organization fulfills a different but important need. ProVisors is the umbrella group for more than 4,000 professionals. At the same time, members have organized other groups outside of ProVisors. One type is masterminds, which comprises 6- to 10-person groups, similar to those formed by Dale Carnegie and Benjamin Franklin. One purpose of such a group is a focus on sharing technical information in a certain area (e.g. estate planning). Other smaller groups might simply contain those persons who regularly refer one another. Another type of smaller organization could group individuals of a particular affiliation, say UCLA alumni.

Forming a sub-group can have a significant impact on your business. At the same time, these "stand-alones" usually disintegrate after a few years. The format and people need to be continually refreshed. And, the leadership must follow the mission and theme of the group. Most participants want the leader(s) to be the organizational and driving force. They only want to attend and reap the benefits.

12. **Have Fun**. Why do anything that isn't fun? Obviously, you will carefully vet those strangers before entrusting them with something as valuable as your client(s). Look for others who also enjoy their profession and excel at satisfying client needs. Passionate people usually have the most fun, because their engaging personality precedes them.

Life is never too stale if you always have the opportunity to turn strangers into friends and allies.

---

13. **Refine Client Stories**. We often have an urge or need to present to our audience the entire litany of our services, as well as too many statements about the benefits of them. At best, doing this will bore your listener to the point that they turn off to your message. Worst case is they never become an ally.

The old and true expression is "Facts tell, stories sell."

I have taken part in numerous discussions and presentations with company owners, executives, and board members, as well as their trusted professional advisors. If there are more than two of them in the room, then you probably want to bring some written materials. However, the materials or deck are only there to aid the conversation. It should never replace an in-depth question or answer session initiated by you to filter out the real needs of the prospect.

In *Own The Room*, an entire chapter is devoted to presenting in teams. Each person designated to speak may own a portion of the presentation. However, that person must be completely coordinated with his or team participants. Thus, all of the detailed material presented should correspond to the role that person will play in delivering the ultimate service.

Client stories told in the flow of a conversation are the best means of emphasizing a relevant point.

Regarding pitching versus sharing, *Own The Room* gives great advice:

> *In a first meeting or pitch, tell an anecdote relating to the client's issue or concern. Delivering a compelling story of how you solved a similar problem will allow the potential client to identify with the protagonist and put herself in the picture to see how you could best serve her. The story will give the image of you with your shirtsleeves rolled up, actually working in that role. And it will eliminate the need for you to ask for the business.*

Each of us has interesting client success stories. My suggestion is that you take the time to organize the best stories that apply to each of your major services. Develop the key factors in each story and write them down. Then, reflect on and determine the major obstacles your firm overcame, and how you succeeded, especially if there was an urgent time frame for completing the work. After you have created the storyboard(s), practice delivering the story in a concise, interesting manner. And then rehearse it again. Make each story an integral part of you. Anecdotal evidence is the best way to convey your message.

14. When you are in the midst of a presentation, relate the stories that best respond to concerns and questions brought forth by the prospect group. How else might you use the storyboard? You can always share one, or a compacted version of one, in response to a first encounter with a stranger at a dinner party. Everyone will appreciate a good, concise story. It provides a reason for others to connect you with their clients and resources. It also gives you the credibility to relate to and solve client problems. Be a Trusted Advisor. How can you *be* one unless you know the traits of a Trusted Advisor (TA)? A TA is at least the following:

- Empathetic but not obsequious to mostly everyone, especially friends, colleagues, prospects, clients, and other trusted advisors. A TA is capable of carefully listening and understanding a person's needs, fears, and obstacles.

- A go-to person in case of personal trauma or emergency. He may be the person you could call at 3 am to come to your aid.

- Reliable. You would call this person for assistance with any matter, including issues outside the scope of his or her expertise.

- Provides advice upon request, but rarely without some indication that the other party is ready to receive the information. He delivers what was promised.

- Provides advice within a sphere of knowledge, expertise, and experience. This person does not offer suggestions that are clearly beyond his scope of understanding.

- Solution-oriented. He readily calls upon others to solve problems outside of his or her level of expertise. This person does not hesitate to refer competent people to fulfill these needs. He is confident that solving the problem with a good referral is more rewarding than the risk of another person not delivering the requisite service.

- Circumspect about the number and quality of other TA's who have become a part of this person's A circle or core.

- Knowledgeable about one's strengths and weaknesses. This person does not mask his or her shortcomings, but readily admits to them. In short, he is transparent.

- Likeable and collegial in small or large group settings.

- Earns respect of others by his or her actions, words, and deeds. This person is less concerned about how he "appears" than about doing the right thing.

- Attracts other TA's to participate in the tasks at hand. He is flexible enough to try new ideas and get group consensus when necessary.

- Acts in the best interests of the clients and constituents; he can serve in a variety of roles, according to what is needed to get the results. The best TA can act as a visionary, champion, facilitator, mobilizer, expert or other role, depending upon the immediate issues and needs of the person(s) being supporting.

- Gives freely to others, without concern for matching returns; his or her attitude is to make life better for others and to make the best connections that get the other party closer to the solution.

Intuition

How well do you know your intuition — those emotional signals that help you make good decisions? So many people believe they make choices based on some type of thought process, comparing pros and cons. To some extent they do. However, usually our best decisions are made when we follow what our "gut" says. No matter the cerebral mechanics, the most important answers are based on how we feel about the alternatives, or based on our own gut check. And, a major part of that gut check is how we assess and judge the people involved.

In Malcom Gladwell's novel *Blink*, he demonstrates how one's inner self or subconscious affects decisions. He explores how psychological and neurological research is correlated to and confirms the importance of human intuition. His numerous examples help support his concept of "thin slicing." That is, with first impressions and few details, we can determine (about 90 percent of the time) a great deal about a person's personality. One example he uses is a stranger assessing someone's traits by a 15-minute look at his dorm room (could have been an office). Our gut instincts provide the basis for this assessment, even if we cannot explain very well what our intuition is "saying." It is an almost instantaneous, correct judgment that serves us well when it is honed and trained.

"When they show you who and what they are, believe them," my friend, Neil Finestone, says about others. People are not likely to change their behavior. What each of us needs to discover and hold sacred is our internal blink clock. How long do you need to know if you will build a relationship with someone? Of course, we all make mistakes. However, we must be honest with ourselves and allow our intuition to take precedent over conflicting emotions. Our experienced gut is usually right.

Let me give you a vivid, personal example. When I moved to Los Angeles in 1980, I knew very few people. Having acted in high school plays, I decided to join an acting class. At my second class, the teacher matched me for a scene with a beautiful woman named Karen. My first "blink" was that I was going to marry her. More than 35 years of marriage later, I think my gut check was spot on.

Was my first reaction primarily based on the fact that she was beautiful? Probably. After we talked for a few minutes and rehearsed our scene, I was hooked. The big fish was reeled in for good. The more we dated, the more my initial "thin slice" proved correct. In spite of the massive proliferation of technology, personal contact with others is now more important than ever. Technology keeps us in touch, as well as informed. There is still no substitute for meeting someone face-to-face. Get comfortable with your intuition, and this will lead you to success in your relationships.

How Do We Know

ProVisors adopted a motto to explain the process for building relationships. The progression is typically Know, Like, Trust and Refer (K, L, T and R). Unless you are connecting with the same person(s) regularly, the time frame to move from Know to Refer is usually six to twelve months. It takes time for people to get comfortable with other people, so they refer them to their most valuable commodities — their clients.

In many groupings or communities, even though the common bond is being a participant, we usually need time to really know one another. In that sense, the K, L, T, R should be L, K, T, R. We often like (or dislike) someone fairly quickly, even if we do not know them.

What does it take to *know* someone? Do I really know someone if he has not revealed a fear, vulnerability, failure, family secret, or passion? Probably not. At the same time, how much of yourself and your problems or concerns are you willing to share? It is one thing to tell someone general information about our children or spouse, or both. It is another thing to tell something in confidence that you do not want "the world" to know. I believe that only our very best friends (our immediate A Core) need to know some of this "secret sauce."

The people we develop relationships with in our A or B Cores should know something personal about us, so they can better understand and remember us. It is up to you to determine how much of your life you reveal to another person. Trust is an entirely different matter. Most people who trust too easily will usually experience regrets. They have to adjust to the hurt brought on by being overly trusting. My suggestion: Trust, but verify. Many can be given the benefit of some trust, partly as a "test" of how much further you can extend the trust. I want to trust others, as I do not want to withhold and be closed off from a potentially strong relationship. At the end of the day, you will not do business or be a friend with someone you cannot trust.

As an offshoot of the ProVisors concept, my son Justin and his lawyer friend, Kent Seton, started a group called AthletesTouch. AthletesTouch comprises people from a narrowly defined demographic — highly dedicated and skilled former college and professional athletes. As of this writing, the group has more than 300 members in 11 locations, including 8 in Southern California, and San Francisco, Portland, and Dallas.

I have observed that, once an AthletesTouch member decides he likes another member, they immediately talk about doing business. They move quickly through the L, K, T, R spectrum. What is the underlying glue or commonality that allows, and even encourages, the athletes to bond so quickly compared to that of professional service providers without the same intimate link?

That "IT" factor is simple: Each athlete knows the dedication, hard work, and sacrifice required by the other person to achieve a high level of sports success. There is also a base level of assumption that this person was a "team" player and sacrificed for the benefit of his organization (team). If we know and appreciate someone's background and circumstances, we relate much more easily. That early acceptance of another's achievements moves the initial conversation quickly to the referral stage or to finding out how we can help each other.

Networking Into a Specific Company

When you want to access a particular person or company, there are a few basic approaches. They all involve using points of connection, as opposed to the proverbial cold call. On the other hand, I know one person (let's call her Sara) who makes not cold but "frozen" calls, or those calls that are directly made to the C-suite (CEO, CFO and COO) level person she wants to reach. Her boldness often works, especially if the executive is a male. Her disarming first salvo is, "Hello X, I am a cure for the common cold call." As she related to me, a friendly conversation often ensues. She briefly touches on her services. Then, she adroitly shifts to the fact that she is not calling for herself, but to ask if she can introduce that executive (X) to an expert (Y). She pauses for a response, which is typically covered by X in his firm. Her next retort is what she knows about his firm that led her to call him. Another pause. At this juncture, if X softens, she suggests a brief meeting time, followed by an exchange of emails (assuming she did not already have his contact information).

Internal networking in an organization is crucial to establish relationships and collaborations.

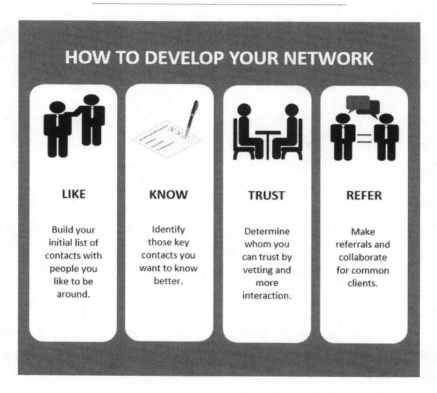

Sara told me that once she hears X answer, she has about 10 seconds to establish some rapport. She is not selling but informing the other person. Better yet, she is offering an introduction of value. Whether the value of the payoff is evident, X remains uncertain. The excitement for her is the challenge of getting a meeting scheduled.

Most of us do not have the chutzpah, time, or inclination to do what Sara routinely does. If she does not reach X, she leaves a short message. However, she never expects a callback and assumes she will call again at a later time. What I suggest is to hire a Sara-type as your intern. More often than not, this talented person will arrange some meetings. Sara's technique is to introduce someone else and attend the meeting as a bridge. She is establishing herself as a trusted and giving advisor.

Your intern may not be well-versed in your service offerings or making introductions. However, if well prepared, he should be able to create a few face-to-face sessions by explaining the basics of your firm's capabilities. Again, your intern should do some research on the prospective firm, such that he can mention that you have some clients in the prospect's industry or another connection to your company.

In regards to Sara, her approach is very unique. But what is the downside to what she does? A hang-up or quick rejection. What are the positives? If rewarded, she has a potential prospect, and kudos from the party she introduces. The only real downside is the time she consumes in researching her targets and getting through the clutter (i.e. the gatekeeping assistant) to actually conduct her 30- to 60-second personal contact.

One of the best ways to engage with a corporate executive is to find a person on LinkedIn who is connected to him. Also, do you know his key vendor, professional advisor(s), friend, or neighbor?

An email campaign can also be effective. This approach can take a few different forms. One is an email blast to members of your network organization, asking for help in connecting with the person or company target. Always share the reason you specifically want that introduction.

When my daughter interned for my company, she researched the CEO or CFO and the firm. She found links to their college, grad school, associated persons, etc. She referenced this "linkage" in an email she crafted to him or her. She then asked for a preliminary or brief introductory meeting. She got excellent results for us, resulting in three engagements within a two-month span.

Another good source of access points are your clients, especially those whom are very satisfied with your recent service(s). There is nothing wrong with asking them if they know anyone whom you should meet. Happy clients are the best testament to your services.

When you read, hear, or learn about something impacting a specific company that may be the ideal time to connect. For example, if the company recently purchased real estate, our firm can send them information about our cost segregation service. The engineering analysis we perform to separate personal property costs from the building results in generating extra tax depreciation in the earlier years. Since depreciation is an expense, the federal income tax payable is reduced.

Another approach upon hearing new information about a specific company is to go to an event or function where someone from that firm is likely to attend. Ask trusted advisors from that firm about how to best insinuate yourself into the firm. Perhaps they will make the right personal introduction. If the event is a gala social or charity function, tread lightly. A very casual approach is best, especially if you can offer something of value, such as a key introduction to another firm.

If you cannot intersect with someone in the C-suite and you are intent on connecting with the firm, try an entry with a lower-level manager. Keep talking to others in the company as to why it is an excellent fit for your services. You just never know when or where a "pair of ears" hears you and is a direct link to your prospect.

Internal Networking

If you are a professional service provider, have you fully accepted your role? Embrace it, no matter what your level, position or title: you are always representing yourself to the best of your ability. The central theme of *The Startup of You* is that the employment progression within your current firm is different today than even the year prior. Social media and the ability to connect to numerous people outside your firm is changing rapidly. Since most of us are mobile, we are all participants in this path of change. Be an "agent of change," helping others seek and reach their professional and personal goals whenever you make connections. They often remember your acts of kindness and generosity. You may not even remember how you helped, but the recipient will certainly never forget.

If you are in a mid-sized or larger manufacturing or distribution firm, there are also internal alliances that can and should be built. Your current job may be gone or could have changed radically in a short period. Will those inside the firm be able to help with future employment? Can you add value for them? If you have a direct sales position, your outside contacts may be invaluable to others. Meet as many of your firm's vendors, professionals, and competitors as you can. Industry groups and associations are ideal for these connections. To become an "agent of change," coach others to stay alert to competitive and industry news, not just rumors. Make time to meet with C-suite persons, both inside and outside of your company. Find out how they view their firm and industry. Determine how you can be a liaison to management, assuming that is where your career is headed.

If you are already in the C-suite, organize internal groups of people to meet regularly, (e.g. biweekly, monthly). Rather than a department meeting or orientation, mix up the employees. Finance/ accounting should meet with sales, engineering, distribution, and manufacturing personnel. Each group should include a mixture of varying personnel, from administrative assistants to upper management. Keep the meeting short and set an agenda, primarily to have someone facilitate the discussion. Topics could range from inter-department coordination issues to suggestions to improve throughput and deliveries. As part of the meeting, you might allow for personal sharing of particular problems and solutions.

With my background in enhancing personal and business relationships, one particular client asked me to participate and provide their management with feedback. So I attended two different sessions of smaller groups as previously described. Each group was given the ground rules that encouraged openness to all comments, as well as a certain expectation of confidentiality.

At best, each person was asked to present something that would benefit someone else. The giving spirit took hold, and employees even requested more frequent meetings. As I understand, morale was improved and "turf battles" between departments were minimized, versus the environment before the institution of the internal meetings. At times, vendors were asked to participate, further improving the dialogue. In essence, this client instituted the power of a community focused solely on the participants. The company benefits were significant based on the camaraderie created within this safe group setting.

Your Marketing Plan

The best plans are often those committed on paper. Write down your target market and how to reach it. The more granular your plan, the more opportunities or pathways you may find.

If you're a C-suite executive but not in a professional service business, do you even need a plan? I believe so. I recently had lunch with a retired CEO of a large, public company. This firm experienced meteoric growth and substantial profitability. A few years ago, their market shifted seismically, and the company filed for bankruptcy. This person, let's call him Richard, was asked to stay on throughout the bankruptcy. Eventually, the company emerged from Chapter 11 and resumed normal operations. Richard remained until the board and his successor felt comfortable with his departure.

Richard admitted that he never thought of forming, joining, or developing a networking community. That "looking outward" never entered his mind, nor had anyone ever suggested it. As I explained my-networking-for-everyone premise, Richard acknowledged that he too was once "naked without a network." Further into our conversation, he reflected on how different his life might have been had the board fired him before he resigned. He also said that, while less important to him now, he fully intended to get involved in one or more communities.

My contention is that the right connections and groups only enhance us. They can make us thrive. In the professional service world, the marketing plan is extra critical. And the beauty is that the plan is intrinsically yours. Customize what is important to and for you. It should define the geography, type(s), and size of potential clientele. Your plan is "living," meaning that it should be referenced often to account for market and firm capability changes, and also your evolving role(s) in the company.

Part of the plan would be a discussion of the strengths and weaknesses of major competitors. In addition, you could determine competitive alliances and how to facilitate these, especially if your firm has client conflicts. Establish the three cores of referral sources, from A through C. Determine how you will maintain your contacts (e.g. social media, email, etc.), including the frequency or cadence. To be more specific, layout a schedule of how often you intend to see your A's, and approximate time frames to meet with the B's, and so on.

Other contacts that you want to cultivate include past and current clients; media personnel; charities; centers of influence; industry associations; business or industry seminar attendees; and weaker ties that can catapult themselves into your B or even A categories.

Highlights

1. Play to your strengths, which should include active listening, empathetic questioning, and helping others with something tangible.

2. Learn more about your personality preferences and style and how to interact best with the other styles.

3. Practice how you want to present client anecdotes, particularly how you solved a difficult problem and produced significant benefits. Have a short client story available for each of your primary services.

4. Know how to be referable by different kinds of people. You must earn and re-earn their respect.

Chapter 9

NAKED NO MORE

We cannot all do great things, but we can do small things
with great love.
—Mother Teresa

Just like everyone else, I have experienced unavoidable ups and downs. The key is to survive and thrive from the lowest points. Our failures are where we learn the most about how to be successful. If nothing else, a failure should teach us how to handle our mistakes, and more importantly, how to handle our next success. A failure also should produce a certain amount of humility. What it should never do is knock us off our game for too long.

One of my major disappointments in life was not reaching the major leagues as a baseball pitcher. At the age of five, I remember the dream to pitch in the Big Leagues. Through Little League to high school, I was a good position player but a better pitcher. Our high school was Gary (Indiana) Horace Mann.

When Charley Finley bought the Kansas City Athletics in 1960, he donated the old uniforms to our high school team. His son attended our high school. Playing my senior year in those major league baseball (MLB) uniforms was awesome, though the pure wool was incredibly itchy on hot days. That year, we won the state baseball championship, and I was our best pitcher. I threw a 92-93 mph fastball and a good curve, but never developed a change-up pitch. The key to a successful pitching career in MLB is throwing strikes with a change or off-speed pitch. I did not know that in high school.

As a freshman at Dartmouth, the varsity baseball coach (also my freshman basketball coach) used me to demonstrate pitching form to a group of local high school coaches. He obviously had very high hopes for my varsity baseball career.

In my first few pitching starts on the freshman team, I was wild, ineffective, and frustrated. In fact, I pitched so poorly that I lost most of my confidence. My coach lost confidence in me as well. Relegated to the end of the bullpen, I saw very little action that year or in any of my varsity years.

So much for the dream to pitch in MLB. Fortunately, I salvaged my sports passion through basketball. I was an All-Ivy player for three years in basketball. But I knew there was no chance of my playing in the NBA.

Life is Fair

Among the better self-help books is *The Power of Who*, by Bob Beaudine. He is one of the most influential people in sports and entertainment. As head of one of the nation's leading executive recruiting firm, he has placed many top executives.

The thesis of the book is that you can create your own job. You just need to execute a carefully crafted plan that taps into your already established network of relationships. Beaudine put the magic number (refer to the *The Magic Numbers* chapter) for his A Core at 12. He terms this the "Who Network." His contention is that your best friend, your BFF, is one of the 12. Next in order of importance are your three closest friends, family, or relationships. The remaining eight are well-known and mutual connections, who are also key to building your network of success.

In other words, decide who is part of your inner core and tell them how to help you find your dream. Each person in the Who

Network of 12 has their own Who Network. The outreach is exponential and endless. The keys are (1) determining your core 12; (2) clearly defining your passion(s) and what you want, (3) listening to what people in your core need; and, (4) narrowing the contacts to those with the best and most direct possible outcomes.

The Who Network, while mandatory for job or opportunity seeking, applies to any position when it comes to building a viable network. The application (and unfortunately there isn't yet an app for that) is different for each individual. But establishing a plan and completing all of the steps is the key to your eventual success.

Modeling for Children

One of the most critical lessons is the power and fulfillment that comes from close relationships. To quote Beaudine, "Running faster and harder all alone is clearly not a good strategy."

I am a big believer that, to a large extent, our children will model the behavior we exhibit and live.

My four children, now all adults, learned quite a bit from me about relationships. They knew some of my struggles and the better successes in building ProVisors. When each was a junior in high school, I invited him/her to visit the local group that I led. Like other members and guests in attendance, each had the opportunity to stand and introduce himself or herself to those in the room. And I asked each to tell the room something about himself or herself. Interestingly, at least to me, was that each child was very poised for a teenager.

After the meetings, they would give me their impressions. Each of them said they felt a strong connectivity among the participants.

I was happy that each one could share the camaraderie created by a cohesive, energetic, caring group of business people.

At various times in their lives, three of my four adult children have either asked for or accepted my offers to connect them to certain people. The fourth, however, is determined to create his own network of connectivity, building relationships on his own. More power to him. However, to paraphrase Beaudine, why race alone when others are willing to run with you?

As a father, I modeled my parenting to teach about the importance of early friendships and fostering those relationships in a career setting. Crucial to that model was the aspect of giving to others. Reflecting on the findings of author Adam Grant, selfless giving to others is not the enemy of productivity; rather, it is the true essence of one's raison d'être. His act of giving is motivating and inspiring, which increases creativity and productivity. Grant believes he is a better person for helping others, and that a sense of service is the greatest untapped source of motivation. We inspire ourselves as we inspire others. Still, the "doing" is the takeaway, not just the *idea* that we want to help others.

The Process

Returning to the prior discussion of "real work" and "net work," there is no *one* way to build your professional relationships. How much and how often you spend time in each kind of work may depend on your personal preference, or what your superiors allow. While each person will find his comfortable pattern, that pattern must continue over time to maintain your relationships. Business development is an ongoing process. One good approach is scheduling a meeting at least one to two weeks in advance. Last-minute arrangements will often result in missed opportunities, as most business people are simply too busy to have much available time in their day.

I suggest that your master networking plan and process involve the following:

1. Review it with an experienced networker for input, perhaps with a mentor.

2. Find a friend to participate with you, which includes attending mixers and group meetings.

3. Continually refer to the plan to reflect on changes you might incorporate.

4. Establish blocks of time for meetings that do not interfere with your "real work." Remember, daytime hours are best for personal meetings. "Real work" can be done before or after the normal workday, or later in the workday.

5. Set specific goals, such as X number of lunches per month when you do not eat alone.

6. Target the number of referrers/resources/associates you want in your A and B Cores. Establish time frames for fulfilling the core numbers. Yet, remain open to adding key persons to each core, especially the A list. Also, be willing to move players off the A list, as necessary.

7. Ask questions about the successes and failure of others. We can learn a great deal from them, since no one has all the answers. Willingly share the nuances and actions that have worked for you.

The only things within our control are our own feelings and actions. The sooner we understand who we are (I AM), the faster and easier we can select a path or plan for building meaningful connections. In some cases, as Beaudine says, "we already know our special core." While he starts there, I personally believe an A Core of 12 is too limiting. We can connect with and learn something from new people every day. Perhaps the "learning from" is too underplayed. I have a simple rule of life: Learn one new thing each day. You never know when you can or will use it.

The 16 MBTI Types

ISTJ

Quiet, serious, earn success by thoroughness and dependability. Practical, matter-of-fact, realistic, and responsible. Decide logically what should be done and work toward it steadily, regardless of distractions. Take pleasure in making everything orderly and organized – their work, their home, their life. Value traditions and loyalty.

ISFJ

Quiet, friendly, responsible, and conscientious. Committed and steady in meeting their obligations. Thorough, painstaking, and accurate. Loyal, considerate, notice and remember specifics about people who are important to them, concerned with how others feel. Strive to create an orderly and harmonious environment at work and at home.

INFJ

Seek meaning and connection in ideas, relationships, and material possessions. Want to understand what motivates people and are insightful about others. Conscientious and committed to their firm values. Develop a clear vision about how best to serve the common good. Organized and decisive in implementing their vision.

INTJ

Have original minds and great drive for implementing their ideas and achieving their goals. Quickly see patterns in external events and develop long-range explanatory perspectives. When committed, organize a job and carry it through. Skeptical and independent, have high standards of competence and performance – for themselves and others.

ISTP

Tolerant and flexible, quiet observers until a problem appears, then act quickly to find workable solutions. Analyze what makes things work and readily get through large amounts of data to isolate the core of practical problems. Interested in cause and effect, organize facts using logical principles, value efficiency.

ISFP

Quiet, friendly, sensitive, and kind. Enjoy the present moment, what's going on around them. Like to have their own space and to work within their own time frame. Loyal and committed to their values and to people who are important to them. Dislike disagreements and conflicts, do not force their opinions or values on others.

INFP

Idealistic, loyal to their values and to people who are important to them. Want an external life that is congruent with their values. Curious, quick to see possibilities, can be catalysts for implementing ideas. Seek to understand people and to help them fulfill their potential. Adaptable, flexible, and accepting unless a value is threatened.

INTP

Seek to develop logical explanations for everything that interests them. Theoretical and abstract, interested more in ideas than in social interaction. Quiet, contained, flexible and adaptable. Have unusual ability to focus in depth to solve problems in their area of interest. Skeptical, sometimes critical, always analytical

ESTP

Flexible and tolerant, they take a pragmatic approach focused on immediate results. Theories and conceptual explanations bore them – they want to act energetically to solve the problem. Focus on the here-and-now, spontaneous, enjoy each moment that they can be active with others. Enjoy material comforts and style. Learn best through doing.

ESFP

Outgoing, friendly, and accepting. Exuberant lovers of life, people and material comforts. Enjoy working with others to make things happen. Bring common sense and a realistic approach to their work, and make work fun. Flexible and spontaneous, adapt readily to new people and environments. Learn best by trying a new skill with other people.

ENFP

Warmly enthusiastic and imaginative. See life as full of possibilities. Make connections between events and information very quickly, and confidently proceed based on the patterns they see. Want a lot of affirmation from others, and readily give appreciation and support. Spontaneous and flexible, often rely on their ability to improvise and their verbal fluency.

ENTP

Quick, ingenious, stimulating, alert and outspoken. Resourceful in solving new and challenging problems. Adept at generating conceptual possibilities and then analyzing them strategically. Good at reading other people. Bored by routine, will seldom do the same thing the same way, apt to turn to one new interest after another.

ESTJ

Practical, realistic, matter-of-fact. Decisive, quickly move to implement decisions. Organize projects and people to get things done, focus on getting results in the most efficient way possible. Take care of routine details. Have a clear set of logical standards, systematically follow them and want others to also. Forceful in implementing their plans.

ESFJ

Warmhearted, conscientious, and cooperative. Want harmony in their environment, work with determination to establish it. Like to work with others to complete tasks accurately and on time. Loyal, follow through even in small matters. Notice what others need in their day-to-day lives and try to provide it. Want to be appreciated for who they are and for what they contribute.

ENFJ

Warm, empathetic, responsive, and responsible. Highly attuned to the emotions, needs and motivations of others. Find potential in everyone, want to help others fulfill their potential. May act as catalysts for individual and group growth. Loyal, responsive to praise and criticism. Sociable, facilitate others in a group, and provide inspiring leadership.

ENTJ

Frank, decisive, assume leadership readily. Quickly see illogical and inefficient procedures and policies, develop and implement comprehensive systems to solve organizational problems. Enjoy long-term planning and goal setting. Usually well informed, well-read, enjoy expanding their knowledge and passing it on to others. Forceful in presenting their ideas.

Excerpted from Introduction to Type *by Isabel Brigs Myers published by CPP. Inc. Used with permission.*

- Appendix B -

NETWORKING TIPS

- Avoid the temptation to consider every contact you meet as a referral source.

- Referrals are made only to those who give as well as receive.

- Some in position to make referrals lack confidence in their ability to judge your ability. Develop their confidence in you through citing mutual acquaintances who know your work, clients, articles written, etc.

- To stimulate referrals, you must be enthusiastic and confident in your work, as well as demonstrate strong ethics, standards, and unique qualifications.

- The referring party must perceive that the person for whom the referral is made will benefit equally or greater than the person to whom the referral is made.

- Prospects for your services are potential referral sources, just as referral sources may also be prospects.

- Current clients are an excellent source of referrals and add-on business.

- People from your past can make good referral sources – former classmates, teachers, professors, co-workers, vendors, clients, and contacts from trade, civic, charitable, and professional organizations.

- Cultivate referral sources with broadcast power. Those in a position of influence or authority — network and association executives, editors, conference chairs — can magnify referral opportunities significantly.

- Identify press contacts in media pertinent to your prospects and referral sources. The press may also identify you as a source of information and contact you as an expert.

- Identify people of great importance or influence that you don't know. Request their participation for an article or research project you're doing as a means of meeting them.

- After meeting a good referral source at a mixer or meeting, promptly send an email. When feasible, connect them with someone who is directly aligned with their business or a resource.

- Prompt your competition as appropriate for referrals, subcontract work, or joint projects. You'll receive referrals and work in return.

- Depending on the relationship, it's sometimes advisable to talk with a party before you make a referral to them.

- A referral is more effective if the referring source contacts the prospective client and suggests that the potential client contact the party being referred.

- After receiving a referral, keep the party making the referral in the communications loop.

- Call, email, or send a written thank-you letter to any source who has referred you.

- Categorize referral sources — potential and actual — into primary, secondary and tertiary groups. Vary the nature by frequency and type of interactions for each category.

- Contact all referral sources at least once every 180 days. Monthly personal contact is advisable for primary referral sources, as are periodic one-on-one meetings. The objective is not to press for referrals, but to maintain awareness and develop relationships, as well as learn new information that is useful for your clients.

- Each member of middle and senior level management should join at least one organization.

- Uncover needs for your network contacts among your client base by asking them if they appreciate their professional advisors.

- Develop a complete referral tracking system.

- Start your networking now. It is never too soon or too late.

- Make it a conscious choice, one you control. Know what defines you and who you are, not just what you do.

- Keep your first impression short and memorable. The elevator speech should encapsulate you and your services in only a few statements.

- Get out from behind your computer. This is a contact sport.

- When you connect with others, you further "your brand." The most valuable asset you own is *your brand*.

- Listen, listen, and listen. Share, share, share.

- Build your alliances so that you become the Venn diagram intersection, or nexus.

- Do not sell, but clearly define and ask for what you want and expect from a relationship. Be directly subtle.

- Specific gratitude and responsiveness to another shows the value you place on that connection.

- Timing is everything. There are times not to network.

- No matter the business, people do business with people. Foster some form of personal touch.

- Show up, consistently.

- Focus on relevancies and commonalities of each other, and remember factoids from prior contacts. Don't start from scratch.

- Warmth is not just your body temperature, but the genuineness you convey.

- Consistently practice acts of kindness and generosity.

- Humor, combined with a serious intent, is never over-rated; it is a winner.

- Rethink the value of your relationships, and re-double your effort on the most important ones.

- Networking is a long-term process. Make it a lifestyle and your life will have more style.

WHAT NETWORKING IS NOT

1. Not direct selling, but marketing

    a. referral sources should not feel threatened

    b. very much like forming a friendship — only a business friendship

    c. should get you the best possible opportunity with the prospect

2. Not withholding information

3. Not about groups, but about individuals

4. Not making promises you won't keep

5. Not going to functions and not working the functions

6. Not being unresponsive

7. Not taking, taking, taking

8. Not expecting an immediate payback, since it is a long-term program

9. Not politics because it is being forthright

I AM- "Davis Blaine"

- Centered, positive, and consistent

- Family man, deeply devoted to my wife and children

- Entrepreneurial, relishing in the vision, creation, building, and success of startups

- Listener first, contributor second

- People person, not a pleaser but a giver to others

- Passionate and committed to causes and ideas that benefit others

- Believer in individual rights and freedoms

- Avid sports fan for my teams

- Control myself and my actions, not actions of others

- Comfortable in small or large groups

- Understand others needs first, to determine if I am a part the solution

- Direct communication style; not overly verbose, which can be disarming or off-putting

- Really like humor, and look for puns from what others say or do

- Strong moral compass; believe in God but not organized religion

- Open to different viewpoints, as long as they come from one's truth and not hypocrisy or hyperbole

- Protector of the facts and truth

- Love dogs

- Strive for organized approach to everything, including planning ahead

- Willing to handle problems and confront others when necessary

- Love to win a competition

- Hard loser (momentarily), and yet learn from my failures or mistakes

- Accept criticism when offered in a constructive way

- Positive about the success of others without envy

- Workaholic who enjoys down time that is active, constructive, or purposeful

- Appreciate beauty in people, animals, and the earth

- Stubborn and set in my ways, unless proven otherwise. Know my likes and dislikes, and not shy about expressing them

- Disturbed by those that do not make the most of their talents and abilities, nor live according to a code of ethics

- Curious and invested in learning new concepts/ideas

- Can be short tempered when someone, especially my immediate family, does something I consider stupid

BIBLIOGRAPHY

Beckwith, Harry (1997), *Selling The Invisible*, Warner Books.

Blaine, Davis (2011), *Coach Daddy*, Authorhouse Publishing.

Booth, David. Shames, Deborah. Peter Desberg (2010), *Own The Room*, McGraw Hill.

Ferrazzi, Keith with Raz, Tahl (2005), *Never Eat Alone*, The Crown Publishing Group.

Gladwell, Malcolm (2005), *Blink: The Power of Thinking without Thinking, Little, Brown and Company.*

Gladwell, Malcolm (2008), *Outliers*, Little, Brown and Company.

Grant, Adam (2013), *Give and Take,* Penguin Publishing Group.

Hoffman, Reid and Casnocha, Ben (2012), *The Start-up of You,* Random House, Inc.

Klymshyn, John (2008), *How to Sell Without Being a Jerk,* John Wiler & Sons, Inc.

Misner, Ivan R. and M.A., Morgan, Don (2000), *Masters of Networking*, Brad Press.

Saleebey, Bill (2009), *Connecting: Beyond the Name Tag*, Believe Publishing.